The Brahma Mind-Primary Force of this Universe

Part – 1

Getting clarity about the secret of the mind.

The consciousness of the universe expresses creation through the Brahma force.A very good book for clarification about it.

C.Poongavanam.

Dedication:

This book is dedicated to God.
A, as its first of letter, every speech
Maintains;
The "primal Deity" is first through all
The world's domains.

Explanation: As the letter A is the first of all letters, so the eternal God is first in the world. - Thirukural

Enlightenment of seeing the sky in the earth is close to those who have researched and cleared their doubts. (Consciousness and scientific knowledge are the same in this sense).

What a single man qualifies himself for! He is doomed to achieve it.

In every soul lies divine power. - Swami Vivekananda.

What one deserves, there is no one in this universe who can stop him from getting it. - Swami Vivekananda.

Content

Chapter 8:

What is Peripheral Nervous System?

PNS

Chapter 9:

Some more information about the brain.

Chapter 10:

Brain functions depend on these

Chapter 11:

What is a neuron? What is a neuron?

Chapter 12:

What are Neurotransmitters?

Chapter 13:

Action potential

Chapter 14:

Resting capacity (resting capacity)

Chapter 15:

Receptive Capacity: (Receptive Capacity)

Chapter 16:

Knowing about fundamental particles, atoms, and five forces can understand cosmic consciousness.

Chapter 17:

Notes:

Technical terms

Sayings:

Text description:

A lot of research about the mind has been going on for centuries. It will continue to happen today and in the future. Many meanings have come together about the mind. However, if one learns what I am saying here, one will get a wonderful opportunity to know what has not been explored, and what has been explored. It is the mind force of Brahma. However, it is very difficult to attribute the essential of Brahma mind force. There are many studies that have done very clearly about the mind. By these, its characteristic is explained. Brahman is hidden in the mind-mysterious philosophy of illusion. But the majority opinion is that the mind cannot be understood. It is impossible for us to pass through today's modern scientific world without using the best knowledge of our ancestors. It is a very good fact that the greatest philosophers, scientists, and spiritualists have not only realized this fact but also respected them and seriously investigated these concepts and accepted them and in that way have provided the best studies to this world. The power of the mind or the power of the mind of aliens is explained in this book. I am sure that the vision of a better world will be available to human society through this book.

A. Author experience in this book:

This mind is a part of the Universal Mind which is connected with all other minds. Every mind wherever it is actually has this subtle psychic force connection with the world. In South India, they are called fortune tellers. Many to meet him

People from foreign countries had come. He called them one by one and told them about their problems and explained that it would happen soon. But I know that he is in India and those abroad have nothing to do with him. I was shocked at how this happened. I witnessed these events directly before my eyes. Similarly, some people with natural powers have come to know the name of an individual, the description of family members, and what problem they have come for. given the solutions for that. They learn this by interacting with the subtle energy using their psychic powers in nature. This is still happening in many parts of India.

Clerics, yogis, psychics, and all religious healers work by using mental energy. Also, mind transfer, telepathy, magic, and many other innovators are using mental energy integrated with this universe to reveal their powers. Millions of people on the earth we live in have made great use of mental energy and combined it with cosmic energy to create great benefits and some evils for mankind. This mental force is pervaded throughout the whole universe. It gives power to man according to his mental energy if he harnesses it properly. The cosmic power reveals itself to the man who listens to it and makes its subtle nature known. Man does not always stand at a limit, but the man keeps asking questions to discover these new things. We know that cosmic power has a knowledge limit.

The most beneficial thing in today's world is to say something that has never been told before in this world or in the history of mankind. There is no point in repeating what is already known. The reason has already been researched and stated by many. When you talk about something so new that its impact can be a stepping stone to the study of a huge change in human society, it's wrong to speculate about something that doesn't exist. But there is nothing wrong in saying that there will be. It is that spirit of inquiry that has helped human society progress so far.

The Universal Mind selects the appropriate human soul to answer this. This opportunity is given only to those who have a conscious awareness of the real universe. It's not for everyone.

In the ancient book Aintiram, Maya explains the qualifications of a great creator as follows. It also fits perfectly in today's modern times. Philosophers, Philosophers, Scholars, and Multidisciplinary experts describe in a beautiful way how ideas are proposed. That is, the serious desire to perceive the truth as it is; The sense of serenity that appears in that thought; And with that sense of serenity comes great energy. Energy is the determination to stand still. He says that they will realize the true meaning of the book due to the unique merits that are based on the multiple natures of clarity in working and the honesty of the text to the world without contaminating the clear idea.

Many events have happened in my life. What will those who are stuck in a small boat in a storm at sea feel? Similarly, I have been caught in the storm of life, failure, success, stress, pleasure, pain, happiness, likes, dislikes, and all the tribulations of life that a normal human being goes through. However, it cannot be denied that the Brahma instinct has helped me move forward in my life by following all these. A kind soul has bestowed upon me the brilliance of knowledge rare to attain the power of the Brahma mind to perform practical actions. Therefore, I have explained the characteristics of the mind, which has acquired the most subtle energy in my mental force and has become the most mysterious, as a light bulb, a beacon light. As a result,

Brahma mind is the primary force of the universe

I have given you the book.

B. Nature has chosen me to write a book:

Title of the book: Sri Yantra Engraved in America and Its Mystery Explained.

Before writing my first publication, this book, some random events took place. Brahma mental force has prepared me in advance.

In my house, there are tiles embedded in the floor corresponding to the numbers 8 and 16 in Sri Yantra. The stone is engraved with 8 lotus petals and 16 lotus petals with beautiful engraving. The wooden sculpture in the puja room at my house shows Brahma sitting on a lotus vine from the navel of Lord Vishnu in palikonda (lying position). Also, there is an idol of Nataraja performing the cosmic dance (Cosmic) made by Aimponn(five metals). There is an Om-shaped script made of brass. The outer wall is inlaid with 16 lotus petals inlaid with granite stones

The rudraksha necklace worn around my neck is encrusted with a coin (pendant) engraved with the Sri Chakra or Sri Yantra and the letter Om (pendant). Sri Chakra engraved coin (pendant) when Kanchi came to Kamatshyamman temple after darshan. A friend of mine kindly provided this. Could the power of this combination be a factor in writing the Sri Yantra book? Was the seed of this sown in my mind? It is actively created by the forces of nature. So I consider writing about Sri Chakra as a command to gain cosmic power.

Suddenly the role of the writer enters the number and leads the way. What I could not do in the previous birth, I get help to complete in the present birth. Through this book, I have given many new ideas. I think it is derived from cosmic consciousness.

Intrinsic event for new work on Mind force:

The work of cognition is to analyze the elements, parts, external processes, and external pre-existing principles of what it investigates, and to explain their relations and functions. And the supreme and profound truth cannot be well understood unless aided by the knowledge of a higher being, whose intellect and reason are not its own, its inner meaning and truths, or even the truths immanent in its external principles and practices. What you need more of here, however, is a kind of visual awakening, an inner visual state, to answer the soul's interview question. Reason always examining from the outside cannot give this inward and intimate connection. It may arise automatically from the Brahman mind force as an aid to your soul power. By a very direct intuition, it will flash to itself the concepts of your knowledge. In this case, my new creation is a revolutionary concept with the slogan of mind as the primary force. I declare the freedom of my individual knowledge, the psyche. Generally, I publish a new set of terms for a new creation.

Also, my analytical reasoning takes things beyond the bounds of normal human reasoning that I have grasped from the Universal Brahman Mind Force. The soul's inner search begins. The understanding of the force of the mind is developed in me by my, awakening of curiosity, nature, rationality, spiritual help, and Brahma mind force help. The light of knowledge that arose in the power of my ordinary mind (this is not spiritual wisdom). It does not come naturally from analysis, nor does it come from a sound and rational faculty of understanding. A higher state arises in the soul by the stimulation of the Brahma mental force, where the light of creation and its power appear and expand in knowledge. It is here that I feel the divine intoxication of my soul. As the assistant of the universe, my analysis becomes the work of this new instinct, the new revelation, the record, the detail, the truth, the commentary, and its expository text reaches its highest peak. It happens in the instinct of my soul mind by grace pretending to be interviewed as an introverted human being. Thus the mystery of mind power is broken or the door to this is first opened with the help of Brahma mind force. It is the secret of the mind's key, practice, content, intrinsic nature, essence, and creation, which, in my view, is released by the rational intellect, a secret more acute and precise.

These events could not have occurred in my life either through senses or knowledge. It is supra sensuous. Although my reasoning and intellect are helpful, I feel that the approaches to this program are supra-intellectual. Here the contact with the force of the cosmic mind, manifesting in my soul and seeing the power, majesty, and character of nature in my mind, I am able to see the true nature of the universe. Therefore, my soul knowledge and truth will help me in the future to find out the secret of the great Brahma and the mind force of man. Divine light, sanctity, and power must come down from above to transform it according to the purpose of our nature to climb up through effort, control, and self-success. Perfect self-surrender is essential. For some souls, this is approved by God.

Preface or Introduction:

A lot of research on the mind has been going on for centuries. This will continue to happen today and in the future. Many meanings of the mind have come. However, few people are aware of this. It is complicated to say what the mind is. There are many studies that have been done very clearly about the Mind. But it is only in the proper communication of this power through the mental force of man that communication movement and creation will come into action.

Pointing out this as the first force in the universe of the mind is a mental force because I am going to summarize in this book what is essential that no one has said before. A number of problems with this synthesis may arise from my definition. I am proudly said of the Universal Mind force is one of the primary +Energy. Wherever the mind begins to act, the Mind force is also in action. The mind and the force of the mind are always inseparable. The mind is a material object and is energized by the power of the Brahma mind. When the mind acts, the mental matter comes into action. Therefore, when it is mentioned that the mind is in some places, we must understand that it is also matching the mental matter or the mental force.

Scientifically, the mysteries of the universe continue to this day. Mind is one of them. However, Yogis and Siddhar are very clearly known about the mind's nature. Some philosophers express their views based on theories. Modern scientific theories, along with modern tools, help to research the mind's feelings in the brain.

Most of the concepts of science, culture, and philosophy expressed in ancient Indian texts and ancient civilizations are consistent with modern scientific discoveries. There may be some differences of opinion, especially regarding the cosmic origin, existence, condensation, sound, light, atoms, five elements, and living beings.

New scientific discoveries happen with the help of today's best philosophers, scientists, ultra-modern microscopic instruments, giant scientific laboratories, mathematical methods, and computers. But in ancient times they discovered new spiritual things through inner awareness.

Nowadays, scientists do not accept all discoveries; especially the ideas and research results expressed by a scientific scientist do not reach complete perfection. From then on, a series of related events take place. At times, it will appear to scientists as a fairly complete discovery. Then many scientists will accept it. They turn out to be a great find. And concern over such findings may not be a purely fundamental objection unless there is a difference in their point of view. Therefore, we know that these kinds of events have been happening continuously since ancient times.

Every philosopher, general science scientist, and individual should respect and accept everyone's principles, opinions, and discoveries as worthy of investigation. Each individual's brain is capable of thinking differently. Therefore, other great scientists should accept those who have new critical thinking skills and knowledge attitudes. No man can be omniscient. Likewise, no nation can become omniscient. Principles and inventions can appear to anyone. This is not only related to science but also applies to any field in the world.

If this is the case with modern inventions, how can ancient ideas accept inventions in modern times? But our forefathers, who are great in knowledge, have expressed many scientific ideas directly and indirectly. Ancient people of knowledge have been researched theoretically and methodically. Our intellectual forefathers have also found success in it. In the same way, modern science also proceeds. I think the concepts of this book will be helpful for cosmologists, science enthusiasts, and researchers. I am sure that the best scientists will feel the old-fashioned nature of this. They should be examined and accepted in my humble opinion.

In general, the note or information of any country is scarce. Even if it is found, its true meaning may not be obtained by not accepting its true meaning or what it conveys as a novelty, rejecting it, and attaching things that do not necessarily fit with them. This pattern is something that can happen in any country. Their intention may have been to cause confusion.

Thus, the difference is made here in the real sense of the thing that can be understood. In this, the troublemakers win and sometimes lose. A close look at world history can lead to brand-new ideas based on old ones. Modern scientific progress has introduced new theories guided by ancient civilizations. There has been better information like this. No one can definitely deny that this has benefited people. It is a well-known fact that a society that accepts the ideas of general change will always go on the path of progress.

Example:

Especially in India, yogis have clearly explained the mystery of the universe, soul, mind, and emotions. No one else could have conveyed these ideas to human society better than them. This choice is made possible through internal awareness and not through external senses. Here, why these should be mentioned is because modern science has been attracted by the interest in some ancient philosophies and human society has reached its present state of progress. No one can deny this. Modern-day scientists like Nicholas

Tesla, Einstein, and many other scientific researchers and scholars have taken Indian scriptures and yogis as references. This led to great scientific discoveries.

Now my point in this book is related to modern science which is completely different from the explanations given in the ancient texts and the new ones. A series of new explorations may arise from this, depending on the impact of my ideas later on. The reason is that when the people of the world pay close attention when announcing a new idea, today's news and related communication tools have the power to reach multiple people. Messages are shared instantly through these modern communication tools. Consent and objections arise. Its impact reaches the whole world in a simple way. Hence, from common people to scientists, these messages are quickly assimilated and their impact emerges. There is reason to mention this here. I hope that such a fast-paced event will bring new scientific researchers from many fields who are interested in learning new things to direct their intellectual vision toward this and bring more facts to the world.

In this book, the understanding of the mind force is explained. So, know about the mystery of the mind force. Author's opinion and also the power of the mind of the aliens speculated and summed up some things, but not the contradictory ones.

My intention in this book is to make certain truths clear to the people of the world like, but not religious views. If such views are not expressed in the book, the true views may not be expressed. The reason is that since ancient times in India, the mind has been revealed or explored through wisdom, so it is obliged to announce it to the world. Even today, clearly proves it based on enlightenment, inner awareness, and meditation.

.

The most beneficial thing in today's world is to talk about something that has never been talked about in this world or in the history of mankind, namely mind force. It is useless to repeat the same thing about the mind because it has already been researched and said by many people from time to time. When you talk about something very new, its impact will be a stepping stone for the study of a huge change in human society. It is this attitude that has helped human society progress so far. The results of this are bound to surprise people. The cosmic mind selects the appropriate human soul to answer this. This opportunity is given only to those who have a conscious awareness of the true universe, but not to all.

Thinking and feeling and writing power

Those who are blessed with honesty and integrity

Perceivers of truth by the ability to know — Mayan's Aintiram

(Tamil Philosopher)

Description:

The serious intention to perceive the truth as it is, the feeling that arises from that thought, the energy that arises from that feeling, the energy that arises from it, fulfill the matter and idea of the book. .-Mayan of Tamil Nadu mentions.

Thirukkural:

Whatever seems to be the nature of anything?

Wisdom lies in seeking to grasp its true nature.

. -423 -Thiruvalluvar

Description:

Whomsoever said it to be something, understand the basic of the that is the knowledge.

Sri Aurobindo explains the glory of intelligence in his book Human Chakra. That is, the work of cognition is to analyze the elements, parts, external practices, and manifest principles, and explain their relations and functions of that which it investigates.

Through the book I sow today, I hope that one day, because of you, the tree of knowledge will sprout and grow into a tree. The one who sows the seed cannot enjoy its fruit. Sometimes it will happen. Then let our posterity enjoy the benefits. Knowledge will expand. This is my intention. But my knowledge is of the encyclopedia of ancestors and also of self-knowledge. No one can get everyone's opinions as a benefit of collective knowledge. In my opinion, this will provide the younger generation with what they need.

This also requires talent, intelligence, creativity, high-mindedness, tolerance, and perseverance. Not all fruit on a tree is good for eating. In which the fruit is affected by various natural conditions before it reaches its normal individual stage. It can be caused by diseases, insects, birds, animals, reptiles, insects, and physical things like wind, rain, and heat. In spite of this, fruits can also happen. The same can happen to humans. In this case, some people like Kai get a creative endowment that transcends various natural circumstances and becomes fruitful. In today's era tree planting is done as a movement and hence there are more available fruits. Similarly, the population of today's people is very, very high. There are also very many people who have the creativity to publish books. Modern technology also helps a lot in this.

It is essential to clarify my ideas and to state many things and methods in this book that are found in other books. As a teacher, I have been trying to understand the nature of many scientific ideas and mention the things said by the ancestors and scientific scholars here and there. I consider this work to be very special to publish new books that are bright with new news and benefit everyone.

What is research?

What is matter eloquence and multidisciplinary knowledge are essential to convey any characteristic of the object of study.

Perpetual telling Power (power possessor) For study selected of substance trait Anything to highlight Versatile Knowledge field Essential.

This is a research paper.

What I Learned:

1. Bachelor of Business Administration.

2. Master of Arts: History.

3. Diploma in Yoga.

4.Divine Will is the Healing—Teaching of Paramahamsa Yogananda.

Edx On-Line Free Courses completed

Science Courses:

1.Introduction to Astrophysics – Successfully completed and passed grade.

2. Evolving Universe.

3. Our place in the universe.

4. Astrophysics: Cosmology.

5. Space conquest: Space exploration and rocket science.

6. From Atoms to Stars; How Physics Explains Our World

7. Cosmic Rays, Dark Matter and Mysteries of the Universe.

8. Big Bang and Origin of Chemical Elements.

9. Astrophysics: Exploring exoplanets.

10. The Greatest Unsolved Mysteries of the Universe.

11. Earth Faith.

12. One planet one ocean.

13. Fundamentals of Neuroscience. Part 3 Brain.

14. Anatomy: Human, Nervous, Anatomy

15. Super - Earth and Life.

Religious Courses:

1. Religious Science.

2. Hinduism through its verses.

General:

1. Public Speaking.

Thank God for helping I write this book.

My thanks to you too!

Chapter 1

In this universe, the primary has appeared as A sense of divine intelligence or Universal mind or cosmic consciousness (cosmic consciousness).

Of the cosmic consciousness High Presence(existence) Very ,Very Mysterious in-depth set up intrinsic If there is the of Evidence basic Enlightenment. Divine Consciousness or Cosmic Mind or cosmic consciousness (cosmic consciousness) from that arose Brahma mind force. Hence, it is a fundamental force. From the intelligence of the universe arose the force of the Brahma mind. in the universe First of all appeared It as the Divine Enlightenment (Parabrahma) or Cosmic Mind. The universal Brahma mind is the absolute cause of all the creations and forces in the universe. The human mind is continuously interwoven with it. The human mind is the physical object. Like space and energy, it is subtle. Universe for the whole match if you see, to the creation of source The reason is That of Moola Prakriti It is the knowledge. Universe About the have Very higher Comment what? What is human understanding of the Universe? Everything Knowledge that's it and that, of the universe areas Everything Kill one together with are functioning. In ancient times this of knowledge expression Regulation of policy by to explain trying there are. Since the beginning of time, the sages have seen the cosmic mind and realized its subtlety. The mind of Brahma can be considered as the force of the mind.

In the beginning That Knowledge Condensed There is At the end It is Absolutely spread out is standing. Therefore in the universe emerges running having Knowledge. The whole thing Universal For appearance Causative First In the contained knowledge in detail is. Since the beginning of time

In the period was This Infinite Knowledge That's it is Of course. universe throughout full of This Knowledge First In the Condensed standing Later on himself Reveal with expanded At last Christ the man Buddha the man that As a human being evolving. This cosmic consciousness is eternal without beginning and without end. It has no beginning and no end; otherwise, it becomes an artificial thing. It is always the same according to nature. But when this sense of fulfillment manifests itself, it seems to us an initiation. That's all.

God's consciousness is everywhere in the universe, He knows everything happening in the world at the same time, just as you know what is happening in your body at any time, God is also aware of everything that is happening in His body, the universe. The universe has a mind just as we have a mind. In the individual, there is somehow the same in the universe. Cosmic consciousness has a physical body. Behind it is the subtle body, behind it is the cosmic mind, and behind it is the consciousness of the cosmic self. Behind it is universal knowledge. All these are in nature. Everything is a manifestation of nature. There is no outside of it.Buddhi is the first manifestation of cosmic

Consciousness. 1. In this state of consciousness, 2.The state of no consciousness, 3. The state of beyond the consciousness is contained. This cosmic consciousness creates consciousness and universal matters.

Cosmic consciousness is called Mahat and Buddhi (intellect). From this intellect arise the subtle prana and the Brahma mental force. From this Brahma mind, all the creations of the universe originate. It makes its presence known to us through vibrations, light, and other forces subtle or very subtle forces in the cosmic consciousness, yogis, human mind, etc. When the Om sounds, light energies, and subtle energy combine, the creative engine of the universe begins to operate. Through the self-awareness of this knowledge, material objects, living things, and black objects that cannot be known by man appear. The feelings of the human mind arise from the cosmic Brahma force and are set in motion by vibration, the vibration particles of intellectual energy, or subtle life forces. Yoga sage Patanjali, who is regarded as the father of yoga, asserts that man can unite himself with the cosmic mind through his individual consciousness or inner consciousness. It is closely connected with man's control of his breath and the Rishis of the Puranas knew and realized its subtle nature.

In cosmic consciousness, vibration is light and energy is light, both of which are the most wonderful and amazing among the billions of mysteries of the universe.

He who is one is Shiva (universe) second he is Shakti (energy). It means sound and light are matching. Shakti and Shiva are two together, Brahman who has the triple task of creating, preserving and giving is also three as Thirumal and Urudhiran. He is the four-fold form of creation, protection, bestowal, grace, and concealment, and he is the universal leader. He is the one who exists in the six religious sects of Saivism, Vaishnavism, Sakta, Ganapadyam, Selaram, and Kaumaram. He is the one who is present in the seven worlds and who directs them. The eight gunas are self-realization, love of the pure body, natural consciousness, complete awareness, non-attachment, transcendental vision, infinity, and limitlessness. As Thirumoolar explains the nature of cosmic consciousness.- Thirumoolar, Thirumantram Hymn 1

Two points should be made to illustrate the power of universality. One is the universe as a manifestation of the mind and the other is the sky. Space is the pride that can be known more easily than other goblins. We are in it. We know its existence. It is spread all over this universe. So it can be called an infinite universe. The reason is that the length, breadth, capacity, and hidden power of this boundless space cannot be contained in a single definition. Cosmic rapture is seen throughout this boundless universe. Both of these are mysterious but we have learned about them from yogis, rishis, scientists, and philosophers. In this the Yogis have expressed very clearly the nature of cosmic bliss realized through inner consciousness. Philosophers say that the universe is like this or that it could be like this. Scientists have only discovered a small amount about cosmic matter through mathematics, through their own research, ideas, and through modern instruments. But this too, one from one to the other, the inventions alternately lead to the next step. It is important to note that we are aware of cosmic reality through the instinct of our mind force . This feeling has been known and demonstrated by many yogis. However, the mystery of this sky remains elusive. If you or I start thinking about this, the mind will start getting confused. But the origin of the universe is unfolding before our eyes. Similarly, cosmic consciousness is ubiquitous.

Here I will explain this in a simple, cognitive way so that everyone can understand. There is the sun. There is also its light. Its power is there. We feel it for sure. This sunlight defines the boundaries of our solar system called the Solar System. From the sun, billions and billions of light rays from big to small, its energy, color, waves, ultraviolet rays, and visible and invisible rays spread in space.

Let's put aside thinking beyond the solar system for the sake of illustration. Sunlight is one of the biggest changes we know of in the solar system, especially on Earth. Due to the energy of the sun and specific light waves, specific frequencies, heat levels, etc., all the elements and their transformations like living things have appeared on Earth. Living things use sunlight as food. For plants, animals, and humans, the leaves, seeds, fruits, pods, roots, etc. of the plants grown in the sunlight give way to human food. Animals get food from plants and animals. This is where you need to know one thing. This is due to the infinite mercy of sunlight. This consciousness of this sun is surely reflected in the sun by the grace of the Brahman mental force of cosmic consciousness. Sun gives us breath, food, rainwater, sea, the soil of the earth, the growth of the Earth; dimensional development of life, dimensional view is a factor in many energy activities.

It is well known that without the sun there is no earth. The reason is that the heat of the sun has tremendous energy and effects. If you think about it, it operates according to its own set of rules. Its energy causes thermal motion, and that motion creates a magnetic field. So it protects us from calamities. Also emits X-rays and infrared rays. These have advantages and disadvantages.Protects the earth from that too. Hydrogen, Helium, Oxygen, Carbon, Iron, Neon, Nitrogen, Silicon, Magnesium,Sulphur, etc. is a photospheric compound. These are present in the earth and in living organisms.

A. How does a seed come to life?

Souls, atoms, etc. come together to forms a seed. When the liquid atom in the spiritual water joins with the Guru atom in the soil, the seed begins to come to life with the heat generated by the Bhutha Karya atoms in the sunlight. And various chemical changes occur in those plant cells through the addition of many sub-atoms i.e. elements. Due to this, its taste and color changes. Sunlight is what causes this seed to come to life. The cause of life in the universe is fire and the cause of it is the sun. Here's a great question that gets a proper answer. The question is, did the seed come first? Did the tree come first? The answer is that the seed came first. - Arudperunjyoti Vallalar.

So the greatest yogis say that without the grace of the sun, there is no life on Earth. Science says the same thing.

The universal consciousness is love, mercy, grace, and goodness. He who transcends the sky, the earth, and the vast universe. He is immortal before and after the creation of the world.

Hiller was a Westerner in the Ramana Mandapam asking Lord Ramana what was going to happen to the world. The first thing the Lord usually does is keep calm, you know he doesn't get involved in things like this, but he saw the intensity of his concern and said, look, there is a creator, he takes care of his creations.

B. Manifestation of Universe mind, Mahat is what?

in the universe of Prakriti First expression is Sangyas Mahat They say this Meaning with Divine Intelligence that indicating. Greatest philosophy this is. In Prakriti occur First Change This wit That's it. This self-awareness that I will not tell Consciousness (self -consciousness). Like that, I say self-awareness and consciousness say it wrong. The feeling is a part of mahat in an. Mahat is anywhere full of. Consciousness, no consciousness and feeling past condition And so on Suppressor Just standing is Mahat. Therefore of consciousness, a partial name for this up Does not apply.

For example, In Prakriti will happen some transitions We by eye see understand We take. But Very Subtle Other Some Changes held Color is. it is not shown. These are Two Types Of transitions due to Being One thing. That's it of greatness Universal feeling; of Brahma mind (Mana) force from this that's it appears. The first variation that's it, Mahat.This Mahat I am As a feeling changes. After this, the cosmos stage Indriya and thanmathiraigal emerge.These two things along with We See Asking feeling. This is a matter of the universe. Philosophy Sangya of According to Universal Creative stage this is it. of nature Or of God very very Subtle. No temptation in character from feeling From the position Brahma of the mind force By vibrating true exisitence Meaning, That is Unformed Nature And Universal of power Innumerable Various vibration network or His of thought process containing Formed Naturally was separated. This is it First Expression. In the universe It is Known as Brahma Mana or Brahma mind force for movement primary force. This continuous Energy, Vibration, sound, light, Invisible, And Visible things are made. In thula matters (material) from Subtlety Brahma Very Subtle of the mind's force cause is revealed. - Swami Vivekananda, Paramahamsa Yogananda opinion Adapted N Explanation.

C. Natures of Universal Mind, Self-Consciousness:

The existence of cosmic consciousness is beyond human explanation. It is uncontrollable. It is inexplicable. Hence the ancient Indian mystics called Brahma Nabunsak, which is neither male nor female. Nabunzak is benign. This type was called the Third Paul by ancient prophets. Brahman belongs to the Napun Sak Lingam. There is a beautiful explanation for this. That is it does not mean both or both in one, but only one is sure. Now the duality dissolves. You rise above the boundary of duality. This is why all concepts of God appear immature. It becomes immature and childish.

The universe was created by the mind force of Brahma through cosmic consciousness. There is a thing hidden in the depths of the cosmic mind, very deep, very deep. Its manifestation is its incarnation. We cannot think that it has materialized as objects and persons because we cannot even imagine it and see it. It is the same power that takes form as matter. It is the same power that takes the shape of a person. If that energy is taken as it is, it is not a substance. Neither is this person. It's just that it's a force. Good and evil are mixed, good and satanic qualities are mixed. The Upanishads are about the universe i.e. God. God is the presence here. Being the cause of all. But he is not here. For example as man but all existence says he is. The universal mind or existence or the Lord's form, qualities, voice, and mind are indescribable. He has a big heart. It is also infinite. He has taken as his abode the heaven which is other than evil and imperishable. He has always made the creation and destruction of all the metals of innumerable forms and the innumerable beings that enjoy them as effortless play—cosmic mind or existence as God does not perish. Likewise, nothing ever becomes anything. Its appearance is all we see now. Existence cannot be seen with your eyes. But he can see your eyes. So he hides behind you. It means that it is within you

Indian yogis are directly in touch with him. With their eyes, they knew His grace and Arudperunjyothi (Grace of light) mercy. The universe is a spiral-shaped cluster of billions of stars that we call the Milky Way. It is seen flying infinitely in the sky. There is physical matter, living matter, and many energies. It contains visible and invisible existences within itself. In one place our solar system resides, and in that solar system the earth resides, and on this Earth, human beings with the ability to think and sentient beings reside. No creature in the universe except man has attained his status. Other living beings are at the lower level. We have not yet come to know with certainty whether there are beings superior to us. However, there is also the possibility of being. This is because of the many rock paintings they left behind on Earth, the way ancient civilizations revealed about them, and the strange lines, paintings, and symbols that mysteriously appear on land even today tell us this. Their flights to Earth confirm this. So it is known that there may be aliens or extraterrestrials. Are extraterrestrials inherently superior to us in the universe? Are they in a different kind of dimensional development and evolution than we are? Will they be with like our knowledge or not to be? Are the elementary particles we know made of other substances than atoms? Are they roaming the universe incognito? is a question that still lingers in human consciousness today. They may be browsing undisturbed. Maybe the universe made them that way. The reason is that the entire universe is still shrouded in mystery. So we should know that anything is possible. Modern science indicates that the unknown universe is full of more than what we know

Those who gave themselves to the Upanishads were rishis who knew the three ages. They are prophets. They were fully aware of the cosmic consciousness. They experienced it as the truth. Their language was very ancient. It is only because race has divided that secret archaic language that it is possible for the secrets of the Upanishads to reach your civilized brain. When something becomes non-existent, it happens when it becomes witchcraft, i.e. what happened to the sage who gave the Upanishad, when you become non-existent, the universal consciousness comes before you and becomes darshan. Lordship disappears when you rise there. It is impossible to talk about pure perfection without experiencing it. It is the rishis who can explain its existence to you through the senses of the Upanishads.

That feeling is called enlightenment in India.

Upanishads are very simple and honest heart-to-heart. It is not philosophical. It is religious. It has nothing to do with principles, theories, or interpretations. It deals with the truth that a man has lived and experienced and that sense can only be gained by experience, not thought.

Atom-to-atom is microscopic

Consciousness itself becomes perfect

Sensing is the intelligence of our Lord

A knowing Consciousness has become the God in the physical universe.

Description:

As inner consciousness and the higher level of consciousness as memory, the mind examines the knowledge, knowledge, or understanding of Shiva Param (God) material (universal enlightenment) even though it is mixed with living beings so, he is everything. He is also susceptible to knowing. However, Thirumoolar mentions that he also exists in the universe as a body and consciousness.

The great power of universal consciousness was called Satya Jyoti and Divya Vijna Jyoti (Truth Light or Supramental Light) by the penance of Mother –Sri Aurobindo Ashram.

The divine light that they say has been brought to this world since February 29, 1956, as a continuous flood of light.

This is what Gnanaprakasa Vallalar says as Arutperunjyothi.

The Vijnana Bhairava Tantra enunciates a different perspective on the mind.

Wherever the mind goes, whether outwardly or inwardly, i.e. towards the inward state, it finds nothing but the state of Shiva. It is omnipresent, so the mind can go elsewhere. Though the awareness of the omnipresent Lord manifests through the sense organs, the sense object (as that awareness) is thought to be of the same nature.

Certainly, man cannot go anywhere else from the cosmic state of consciousness to any Brahma force.

(Just as the River of Cosmic Consciousness has a source, the River of Consciousness also has a source. It comes from Cosmic Consciousness, the consciousness of God beyond all creation, and Super-Consciousness or Soul Consciousness. When the Christ Consciousness descends into the soul and pure mind of man, it is called Super-Consciousness). Paramahamsa Yogananda says.

D. universe poem:

Enlightened Universe

Consciousness Universe

Non-understandable Period Universe

You are That's. it is the Universe

Singularity Universe

Mind Universe

As power Universe

Nathem (vibration,or sound),

as the Vindu (Energy+Light) Universe

Vast Universe

Strange Universe

Archaic Universe

In the cycle of time Universe

Border unseen Universe

Prana power contains the Universe

Black Energy possesses the Universe

As the soul Universe

Self Conscious Universe

Infinite Energy Universe

Evolution Universe

Dimension Universe

Light Universe

Sound Universe

Vibration Universe

As frequency Universe

In color Universe

Blue Light Universe

Whiteness Light Universe

Gold Light Universe

Brahma force Universe

Basic particles Universe

Atomically Universe

Giant Space Universe

Loveable Universe

Basic Universe

Formless Universe

The Forms of the Universe

Illusion Universe

Alive Universe

Creator Universe

The Exists of the Universe

Disappearing Universe

Snarling Universe

Flying universe

Spreading out the universe and flaming Universe

Will grow infinity characterful Universe

Micro Energy Universe

In many ways Other than its create a Universe

The Universe spread like a quantity of the viruses

Will spread like a Universe is a banyan tree

Characteristics did not define the Universe

Gold Light shines on the Universe

Appearance can't know the Universe

From the beginning and the end not knowing Universe

Dark and Light-Explained Universe

For yogis Luminous Universe

The Universe is a science to scientists

The universe manifests itself to yogis

Universe Science explains to scientists through external senses

The Universe is hidden in a light

Transcends the cosmos

The universe is vast

The universe turned into fire and smoke

A universe with gravity

An exclusionary (repulsion) force universe

Universe as electricity

The Universe is an Electrostatic force

The Universe has a magnetic force

Universe as lightning

Radiant universe

The refracted universe

The universe of photo degradation

The collective source material universe

A universe that develops like a seed

The universe is like a banyan tree

A universe that radiates reason

The universe that revolves before the eyes

A universe full of mysteries

The universe is like a colorful constellation

A burning universe

A cool universe

The universe that created material things

The Universe moving forward as one within one

The Universe that goes outward as one within one

Hole-dominated universe

A thought-provoking universe

A universe that answers some questions

A universe that helps creations

The Universe has incomprehensible energy

The Universe as Conscious Energy

Justice and Dharma are the Universes

Omnipotent universe

A universe with ten directions

Dark blue is the Universe

The Universe is yellow

The Universe is green

The Universe is red

The Universe is purple

The Universe is orange

The Universe is and blue color

Universe as Pranava Mantra Om

The Universe as Om, Amen, Ameen

Electromagnetic radiation Universe

A universe with high-energy cosmic rays

A universe of electromagnetic waves

The universe is characterized by dark matter.

A universe characterized by dark energy.

Author - C.Poongavanam.

E. A yogi named Vallalar in India, gives the world a new idea about cosmic consciousness.

I have explained his ideas in a modern way.

The first stage is Pathi which means Lord.

Suththa Shivam.

The second stage is the meipathi space.

On the third plane, material and space, the Brahman force is formed into Sat and the mind.

The fourth stage is Chitturu Veli(space) Here the power of Brahma mind reaches the upper mental level called Sidthabo -2. Then in the fifth plane called Paraveli(space), Shiva becomes Shakti.

The sixth stage, outer space, is where the force of Brahma mind reaches the state of Natham (sound), Vindhu (ligth). The Universe becomes matter.

In the seventh stage is the force of the Brahma mind called Satasivam.

In the eighth stage is the power of the Brahma mind called Esvara.

In the ninth stage is Rudra, the force of Brahma mind.

In the tenth stage is Vishnu, the power of Brahma mind.

In the eleventh stage, the power of the Brahma mind, called Brahman, originates.

In the twelfth stage, due to the force of the Brahma mind, the soul, material, darkness, intelligence, and vital material, a small light is formed. periods, causal, and causal phenomena occur.

Cosmic consciousness evolves in these stages.

Period: Pathi means the Brahma force of the mind of the Lord or Aruchsati(energy)and is associated with time. The period of cosmic silence is called the period of motion of cosmic nature. This period of motion includes creation, existence, and condensation. Therefore, God's action is connected with the period.

Eddington, one of the greatest scientists of this age, says, "We used to think that matter was; now it is not. The matter is like a thought, not like a thing."

Chapter 2

What is Brahma mind force? An explanation according to the science of Brahma mind force? What are its absolute proven actions?

The Divine Enlightenment or the Universal Mind is the Brahma Mind Force from which it emerged. The Brahma Mind Force emerged from the Intelligence of the Universe. The Brahma Mind Force that emerges from Prana, the moving force of intelligence, is a micro-force.

An explanation according to the science of Brahma mind force?

According to science, dark energy can be based on muon neutrino, photons. It is the force related to human beings by the mental force of the universe. When the human activates the mental force, it is manifested as electromagnetic energy. The terms electromagnetic radiation and electromagnetic waves all refer to the same physical phenomenon, electromagnetic energy. Black Energy (dark energy) muon, photon is the only physical phenomenon with electromagnetic energy (photons are tiny particles of dark energy).

An electromagnetic wave passes through space and its equation is given by,

E=EO Sin (wt- kx) where E is an electric field.

If you divide mental energy into mind + energy, then the mind is a physical substance and force is energy. For this mental energy to work, you need the brain. Similarly, intellect, mind, ego, and will, these four factors are necessary. Also, by introspection, the mind force is related to the cosmic mind, soul, and body.

Universal Mind+Soul+ Mind Force+Body of Living Beings.

Scientifically, the sense of the brain depends on the individual. It causes the electromagnetic energy of the brain nerves when the senses work.

JohnjoeMcfadden, one of the working professors of the University of Surrey, put forward a new theory about the brain through his research. According to this, the electromagnetic energy in the brain helps to bring about brain functions, our memory, awareness, and thinking ability. – JohnjoeMcfadden

When the waves emanating from our brain interact with the waves outside the space, it is developing as an action. In accordance with the thoughts that appear in the human brain, the respective waveforms and frequencies, electrical communication inductions are defined in the nerve fibers. PV (PARVALBUMIN) in the brain (parvalbumin fast-spiking inter neurons-(PV-F S I) (neurons provide knowledge for something related to various thoughts.

$$E = mc^2$$

Just like the formula, the more energy you create and manifest in the brain as a mental force, the more energy will arrive from the cosmic mental force at the speed of light. The action of these three forces is equal. Mind force is generated when an atomic particle interacts with its associated antiparticles or interacts with dependent particles. Energy and momentum are conserved. Then the particles combine with the electromagnetic waves associated with the photon. Thus, mind force is created.

M=T+EF+ME+MF

M = MIND

T = THOUGHT

EF = ELECTROMAGNETIC FORCE

ME = MICRO-ENERGY

MF = MIND FORCE

I think that the formula is correct. No matter how long or years pass, the energy of this mental force will manifest itself at the appropriate time.

Like other basic energies, the power of the mind becomes energy when it is manifested as a movement. The power of the human mind is very powerful. The Brahma Shakti of existence is uncreated and eternal. The Brahma Mind Force is sophisticated vibrational energy associated with Quantum Electrodynamics (QED), Quantum Entanglement, Grand Unified Theory, Elements, Molecules, Electrochemistry, and Bioelectricity. Universal Brahma mind energy is the absolute cause of all creations and forces in this universe. Cosmic Consciousness as God or Creative Energy creates itself as vibrations and becomes dependent on illusion as Universe, Form, Time, Darkness, Cause, Lord. This is the beginning of Brahma Buddhi. From the mind energy of Brahma, human beings, other living beings, aliens, the senses of living beings, and everything visible and invisible emerge from the cosmic vibrations.

The power of the human mind is constantly intertwined with it. The human mind is the knowledge that provides the Brahma Shakti to this material movement. It's like space and energy.

There are four fundamental forces (shaktis) in the universe. They are gravitational force, electromagnetic force, strong nuclear force, and weak nuclear force. Apart from this, man tries to find new powers. Why shouldn't there be new forces in the universe? This matter may be beyond our understanding. It is beyond human power. Space wave is helpful for psychic feelings. I can be very clear about

Brahma Mind Force.I'm going to make that point. Brahma Mind Force can also be known through this book. The name of that new introductory force is Brahma Mind Force. Like the other four basic keys, this key is related to cosmic energy. So I consider Brahma mind force as primary. It is an amazing power. The key to the human mind is the same as the key to Brahma Buddhi. So, no need for confusion.

What are its absolute proven actions?

The mind force of man and other living beings is a part of Brahma mental force. Generally, the Brahma force does not interfere in the life activities of individual beings. The categories of life, its evolution, its dimensional development, its life pattern, etc. depend on the birth of the respective period according to its karmic fate. But none of its actions can escape the observation of the Brahma mind or mental force or cosmic consciousness for a moment.

There are six basics in this universe namely mind, air, air, fire, water, and earth. It has been said that there have been five basics for thousands of years. But the mind also has the characteristic of being treated as a goblin. The mind is also material like these. All these require prana or Brahma or the material source energy to function. I am going to submit to you a fully substantiated opinion based on the knowledge of our learned ancestors as the basis of the findings of the present scientific world. What is it?

Even today the scientific world is not fully aware of the Brahma mental force. It was the yogis (yogis) of India who explained this power of the mind and its properties with full evidence. They have been teaching about this from ancient times to the present day and are still teaching. I call it the Brahma Mind Force.

Chapter 3

A scientific explanation of the force of the mind?

The mind force of the common man through the five senses (eyes, ears, nose, tongue, body skin Kanmandriyas (hands, feet, speech, genitals, anus)), antahkarana (mind, intellect, ahankara, and chitta) engages in some kind of pleasure feeling, pain feeling and struggle every moment.

It is an individual mental force that struggles with expectations, desires, past, present, and future.

Force vibrations of mind, light, frequencies, waves, electromagnetic waves and energy, quantum entanglement, organisms, thought, consciousness, body and brain, brain waves, magnetic field, physics, chemistry, biology, cosmic black energy, cosmic mind force. is a link.

The force of the mind is more subtle than other basic forces. It can be converted into a thought in the brain and complete an action by the stimulation of the mind. Mental force is a sophisticated vibrational energy, associated with quantum electrodynamics (QED), quantum entanglement, Grant Unified Theory, elements and molecules, electrochemistry, and bioelectricity. Cosmic Brahman is the absolute cause of all creations and forces in this universe.

When a person creates thoughts in his mind and puts them into action, when he thinks and starts to act, the neurons in the brain are activated by neurotransmitters. Here the electrical signals are generated at the corner. Also, active chemical substances are activated in the brain, especially the axon and dendrites, which are surrounded by lipid molecules on the outside and inside. This is called the cell membrane. And the voltage is not neutral when the cell is at rest. But it can be said that there is a voltage. Here, if the potential of electric power is measured inside and outside the membrane, there is a voltage and it is called the membrane potential. This voltage is minus 70 millivolts (-70Mv). Normally, the voltage is caused by chemicals in batteries.

As with neuron activity, there are substances on both sides of the cell membrane. Many of those things are made of water. If they are, there are proteins, ions, and sugars and a whole host of charged ions and molecules, such as magnesium, bicarbonate, etc. are in the field, and floating around are phosphates, sulfates, and other proteins. These chemicals or elements are positively and negatively charged. Charged ions (ions) are present in high concentrations of sodium, potassium, calcium, and chloride. These play an important role in the relaxation ability of the neuron. And these chemicals move inward and outward along pathways in the membranes to and fro in a manner appropriate for specific thought processes. It is suitable for the specific thought-action of the human brain, and electrical signals are generated in the inner regions of the frontal lobe, parietal lobe, occipital lobe, and temporal lobe in the brain-based right brain and left brain due to these actions. Then voltage becomes energy. A particular part of the brain is exposed to certain chemicals or chemical substances. During the events, mind force is formed based on electrical force, electrical signals, brain waves, and frequencies. In this way, thoughts are formed and act in the areas of the brain, and the mental force suitable for a specific area develops into appropriate action. For example:

If you hear a low frequency of 19 Hz you start to panic. You will feel relaxed and calm in the presence of 432Hz frequency. This 432Hz frequency has many healing effects on your mind and body. The human body responds to different frequencies. Our human body vibrates at a natural frequency of 7.5 Hz, which is very close to nature. Did you know that there is a certain frequency associated with an emotion? Emotion is electric+movement.That means energy in motion.Frequency of different emotions. Higher frequency means higher vibration. Correspondence to the higher energy level. Good emotions have high frequencies while bad emotions have low frequencies. In the Enlightenment condition, the frequency is higher than 700Hz. And the lower frequency of vibration is the lower energy, which is equal to only 20 Hz, with the same sensations.

Frequencies like 700 Hz, our mind enters a state of super consciousness. Transcendental consciousness is the blissful state of self-realization. This egoic state is beyond the conscious and subconscious levels of the mind. Friends, I briefly found some interesting things that help us understand life in a better scientific way. Frequencies of peace and desire in particular caught my attention. It has been observed that the frequency of peace is the second highest frequency after enlightenment. It shows that peace is at a higher level than happiness and love. When you are calm, you vibrate at higher frequencies compared to someone who is in love or enjoying the pleasures of worldly things. So it is clear from science that attaining a state of peace is bliss rather than running after worldly pleasures. – Reference YouTube video: Everything is frequency and vibration – emotional frequency.

Note:

Do our bodies have electricity?

Electricity is everywhere in the human body, and our cells are specialized in communicating the current. Elements in our body, such as sodium, potassium, calcium, and magnesium, have a specific charge. Almost all of our cells use these charged elements, called ions, to generate electricity.

The following are scientifically accepted actions of the mind.

1. Manas, Ahankara, Buddhi, Chitta

2. Consciousness, state of unconsciousness

(Unconsciousness)

3. Subconscious mind

4. Awareness

5. Transcendence

6. Presumptive power

7. Fainting

8. Wakefulness.

9. Sleep

10. Dream State

11. Endlessness

12. Seer

13. Thought

14. Actions

15. Change

16. Paramananda

17. Meditation

18. Exciting experiences

19. Using our energy for constructive things

20. Physical energy

21. Psychological power

22. Breath

23. Brahma Force Correlation

24. Human mind force communication

25. Prana communication

26. Parabrahmam communication

27. Super psychic communication

28. Spatial communication

29. Natha level (vibration) communication

30. Atma Siddhi status communication.

31. Knowledge is power

32. Multidimensional knowledge is wisdom

33. Enlightenment

The psychic (mind force) power to cure the disease:

1. Pray to Jesus for healing

2. Reiki and prayer

3. Yogananda's healing prayer

Techniques.

What are the powers of the other senses?

1. ESP (Extrasensory perception) ESP (Extrasensory perception)

2. Intuition.

3. Telepathy

All these arise from the Brahma mind force through the human mind force.

Chapter 4

What was the Brahma mind force of the universe like in the most ancient times?

The consciousness of the universe was in a silent nature of existence and non-existence. Could there have been a situation in which there was no Brahma mental force in the universe? or silent divine consciousness. Do you know the answer to this? Certainly would not have as it is now. But if such a state had this whole cosmic force in it, you cannot believe who has told this. How is this possible which is not possible with the help of modern tools in this day and age? Indian Vedic texts provide an excellent answer to this.

Does it imply that there was an ancient universe characterized by nothingness?

Then there would have been no quantum motion and there would have been no such thing as light-sound and there would have been nothing in motion is not there. A great mental force is silence. This can be called cosmic silence. How many billions of years would this state have been, and could it return? But it is only certain that previously this attribute contained the force of the Universal Conscious Mind. The greatest yogis of India have realized this by relating themselves to the cosmic mind force. It is my opinion that only pure yogis realize this and express their views, and there is no need for doubt in any way. It is described in the Vedas how it is. This is the testimony of this.

I mean, it's still there. It is subtle. The Sangya philosophy states that the cause is in form. Specifically, the Brahma mind, the fundamental elements, are symmetrical in nature without distortion.

(Therefore, the universe must also operate in the same way in the beginning with the subtle form without being known and manifested. We call this state chaos. From that state, the new creation appears. The universe remains in its subtle form for some time and then emerges. This period is a kalpa in Sanskrit which means cycle says) - Swami Vivekananda's Heroic Languages.

Chapter 5

Mind Force can be divided into five types:

1. Divine Mind Force or Brahma Mind Force
2. Yogi's Mind Force
3. Mind force of the common man.
4. Mind force of other beings:
5. Alien Mind Force:

1. Divine Mind Force or Brahma Mind Force :

Consciousness is the essence of the universe. This is the mental force of God or the mental force of Brahma. The Universal Mind can be called Brahma. Brahma is the form of Truth, Wisdom, and Bliss. It is from this that the creations were created. The man named Purusha is also the one who came into this creation. It is the source of knowledge and power for all the energy in the universe and is time, cause, and matter. This mental force belongs to the Universal Lord beyond all. This mental energy pervades the entire universe. It is an eternal force of mind. All the religions of the world agree on this. In Bharat, it is called Purushottaman, Christians call it Paramabita, and Muslims call it Allah.

In the force of the cosmic mind, the first word that appeared was Om. It is energy, vibration, sound, light, wave, basic particles, atoms and related, material objects, living things, galaxies, stars, planets, cosmic sub-objects, etc. in the vast space. The first variation of the real matter was the manifestation of thought. Then from the thought seed of his consciousness came sound (strings), cosmic light. The sensation is the same as light, except that light is slightly denser. The idea of light is subtler than dream light. According to God's mental power, light began to function in the space region of the universe and this light is the of all creation. The power of God's mind transforms the life force into microscopic light, bioelectrical atoms, the smallest and most fundamental elements of matter (leptons and quarks) or combinations of these (hadrons with quarks), and the various fundamental subatomic particles that transmit one of the five fundamental interactions in nature (mental force, gravitation, electromagnetism, strong and weak). And the dense atomic formation of bioelectrical atoms called protons, neutrons, and electrons. God gave these protons, neutrons, and electrons energy. It is through this that they form themselves into atoms and molecules. He described atoms and molecules as gases, heat, liquids, and solids as all creations in his mind.

Where does this universe come from? in which it is established. In the end, it is asked where it goes. It comes from the love of Prana and is established in love. The answer is that in the end, it goes to love.

Sage Patanjali, a legendary Rishi, realized the cosmic energy. He clarifies for us the idea that he felt in his mind. That is, the Patanjali says that Ongar Nath is the universal light (divine).

Aum is the word of creation, witness to the presence and rotation of the cosmic machine. The tremendous power of light emerges from the word AUM which can be produced. It is the energy flowing in waves in the universe that evolves into the energy of all atoms.- Autobiography of a Yogi.

In spiritual books like the Bible and the Koran, we can learn that the Lord created the universe by uttering words with the power of the mind. Here too there are vibrations when words or words are spoken. Therefore, God is associated with psychic vibrations.

The Brahma mental force consists of vibration, light, and magnetism. There is no movement in the universe without vibration, light, and magnetism. All these three are one compound.

According to the theory of quantum entanglement, Brahma mental force and human mental force can communicate.

According to the theory of quantum entanglement, two particles can entangle each other in a certain way, even if they are far apart in space. The great physicists Albert Einstein and Erwin Schrödinger first discovered and announced the phenomenon of entanglement in the 1930s. Through this, there is a definite possibility of contact between the mind of Brahma and the mind of humans. The principles of science are proof of this.

2. Mind force of Yogis:

Yogis are those who have the knowledge of the true nature of the cosmic power, who have fully learned and realized the best knowledge books created on this earth and the Vedanta philosophical explanations, who have attained the qualities of the 64 arts in silent samadhi by suppressing the mind, mixing with the supreme substance of the Lord, and who has acquired the quality of seeing himself as Him. Yogiyavar .-Thirumoolar.

Their mind energy is transcendental, neutral i.e. pure, peaceful, happy, well-being of others, aware of the peculiarities, differences, and pitfalls found in nature and take the best decision about them, and in the form of eternal mercy, they will be at their highest energy level. Those who have spread their mental power, whose power has worked in the hearts of thousands, and who have ignited the spiritual fire in the lives of others, have the mental power of wisdom at its best.

The power of the mind of the best yogis (super consciousness or mental power) manifests as omnipotent power. It has the ability to see, taste, consume, touch, and hear without the aid of external senses, as described in the Taittiriya Aranyakam. The human body is precious. Due to the unique nature of the psychic force which is dependent on the body, it has attained the highest dimensional development with the help of the brain and the centers of the spine through which a yogi can fully understand and express the sublime nature of the divine. Yogis can transform their bodies into particles and waves of light by mental force and travel to the required places and manifest themselves there.

Yogis attain enlightenment by the grace of the Guru. But the qualification to get it is done according to the karma of that soul. Some people become enlightened by the power of the mind in themselves. Yogis attain enlightenment in a state of higher meditation or superconsciousness.

Example: Buddha, Ramana Maharishi, Osho, Jackie Vasudev.

Similarly, many people have witnessed some yogis sitting floating in the air. This is how astronauts in a space station orbiting Earth feel weightless and floating in space because of gravity, the acceleration of gravity being equal to the spacecraft's thrust. Yogis create such a position around themselves and achieve a state of sitting where they can defy gravity on Earth and use their mind power to stand in the distance.

Through the mind power of yogis, in some works, not only the boundaries of the senses are crossed but also the dominance of reason. Then the mind of the yogis sees many blessings that cannot be realized through the senses or through research. The yogi's mind has a strange power to transcend the senses and the boundaries of knowledge. Many yogis have proved this.

3. Mind force of the common man:

The mind force of ordinary people is involved in some kind of sense of pleasure and struggle every moment through the five organs, the senses called Kanmendriyas, and the mind, intellect, ego, and mind. It is an individual force that is fighting fiercely depending on expectations, desires, past, present, future, etc. It works on the basis of the individual ability of each individual. The extent to which one tries to complete the tasks undertaken by him will reveal his ability in his field. This mind direction can be biased towards either of the two poles of success or failure. There is good and bad in it. Always and every moment the mental force of man is a great field of struggle, from which he does not seem to have any escape but to face it.

That which is formed by social structure is the mind. Verily, that which is shaped by such development becomes intelligence. Sri Panchadasi.

4. Mind force of other beings:

The mind power of animals, birds, reptiles, aquatic life, tree, plant, flag, grass, etc. is dependent on survival. It is seen with changes according to the evolution of the respective organisms. The mind power of those animals, birds, used to living dependent on humans is different. The mind power of plant-type organisms is very low. It has vibrations. It is completely different from the connection of the cosmic mind vibration of human beings.

5. Mind force of Aliens:

The mind strength and higher level of aliens are greater than that of Earthlings. According to the nature of mental energy, they hide their bodies by varying the mass of atoms. They are capable of penetrating matter like the Higgs boson particle. They keep an eye on the inhabitants of the earth and visit the earth frequently. We must consider ourselves as having more power and intelligence than our minds. The reason is that a closer look at what has happened on Earth so far reveals a few things. So far, no country in the world has reported accurate information about any disruption caused by them. It is considered to be researchable. This can be traced back to the events that took place in some civilizations in ancient times.

Chapter 6

Brain:

Brain The brain is responsible for an organism's feelings, knowledge, memory, bodily movement, etc. The brain is an important factor in human body functions, as well as the body functions of other organisms. The brain is a part of the body that coordinates various nervous systems. The brain is the chief of the human nervous system. It is the most complex of human organs. The human brain is five times larger than that of other mammals.

It makes other organs in the body work according to the command of the brain. The mind through its power with the help of the brain is responsible for phenomena like our waking state, sleep, and dream state. The brain is an organ that operates with the soul and mind. The human brain is the soul and mind through the five senses namely touch (feeling the body), seeing (seeing with the eyes), hearing (hearing with the ear), smelling (smelling with the nose), and tasting (knowing taste with the mouth). It also works according to manas or consciousness or mind or intelligence, ego, and Chitta. The brain cooperates with every action of man by mental force. The brain is energetic. The brain is an information-gathering, publishing, memory, and coordination center for transforming thoughts, energy, and actions. Electromagnetic energy, electrochemical energy, thermodynamic energy, electrical energy, and energy of the Brahma (universe) mind are formed as brain energy. The brain converts pure mental processing power into energy.

A human brain has about 10,000 crore neurons, which means it is made up of more than 100 million nerves. A microscopic examination of brain tissue reveals a startling fact. There, it can be seen connected by billions of neurons and billions of synapses. The brain can be divided into the right brain and the left brain. These are divided into frontal lobe, parietal lobe, temporal lobe, and occipital lobe. Each of these parts is responsible for a number of specific functions. Likewise, the brain is made up of 75 percent water. A human brain weighs between 1500g and 1100g on average. The brain works using electrical energy. Our brain produces 25 watts of power. The human brain weighs about three pounds. 60% of the brain is fat. The remaining 40% is water and protein is a mixture of carbohydrates and salts. An average person uses only ten percent of their brain. Some extraordinary people especially pure yogis use 100 percent brain power.

Our brain, Brahma force, soul, mind, water, particles, elements, chemicals, electricity, brain waves, brain frequencies, energy, consciousness, and heat are, contained everything compound objects.

The brain has four lobes in the cortex, namely the frontal lobe, parietal lobe, temporal lobe, and occipital lobe.

Frontal lobe:

Memory

Cognition

Thinking

Linguistic thinking

Speech

Touching

Mathematical calculations

Tasting

Making the right decision

Pay attention

Literacy and language learning

Planning

Parietal lobe:

Respond to sensory information. It is essential for emotional perception and coordination. Controls learned movement and orientation. Participates in the activities of the five senses.Specifically, touch, pain, heat, spatial and physical awareness, pressure, vibrations, analysis, recognition, somatic sense memory, and manipulation of objects.

Temporal lobe:

Long-term,with real memories. It deals with sound and language. That is, hearing, learning, facial recognition, object perception, language recognition, control of the unconscious, and apparently automatic reactions such as hunger, thirst, and consciousness.

Occipital lobe:

Receives stimuli, images from the eyes and converts them into information.(Visual processing) Improves memory formation, and intuition. Time, distance, and depth perception, object and face recognition or recognition.

Cerebellum:

Controls body coordination. Enables body balance and eye movement. The human cerebellum is an area at the back of the brain with 69 billion neurons. The cerebellum directs activities in health and disease.

The human brain is divided into the right brain and the left brain. In these, the right brain performs some human activities and the left brain performs some types of human activities and brings energy. In this, the right brain controls the left side body parts and the left brain activates the right side body parts and expresses energy. Each of these actions appears in accordance with human thought and accordingly manifests as instinct and transforms into energy.

Left brain:

Memory power,

Science,

Study,

Logic,

Mathematics,

Calculation,

Thinking of words,

Emotional thinking,

Positive emotions,

Right-sided motor skills,

Immunity

Activates,

Rational thinking

Processing Information

Language

Right brain:

Creativity

Intuition

Complete thinking

Left-sided motor skills

Artistry

Visualization of feelings

Negative emotions

Rhythm

Suppresses the immune system

Music of songs

Multiple tasks

Description of information

Chapter 7

What is the Central Nervous System (CNS)?

The Central Nervous System of the brain is called CNS.

The central nervous system of the brain consists of the brain and the spinal cord. The brain is divided into the right hemisphere and the left hemisphere. The brain is responsible for general functions, feeling, awareness, thinking, memory, cognition, intelligence, emotions, creativity, learning, behavior, empathy, attention, anger, and fear, regulates body temperature maintenance, organ coordination, regulation, etc. The spinal cord carries messages up and down between the brain and the nerves that run throughout the body.

1. Spinal cord:

The spinal cord is the connective tissue at the base of the brain. It is a long spine. It transmits nerve signals from the brain to the parts of the body, i.e. it helps to perceive sensations. The spinal cord transmits nerve signals from the motor cortex for bodily functions. It also functions in the transmission of sensory neurons from the fibers to the sensory cortex. The spinal cord is part of the central nervous system. The terminal end of the spinal cord is the cone medulla. The brain and the spinal cord work together to make the human mind and emotions work better.

2. Brain stem:

The brainstem consists of modules of white and gray matter. The brainstem is responsible for emotions, breathing, blood pressure, heart rate, and sleep. The brain stem consists of the midbrain, pons, and medulla oblongata.

Chapter 8

8. What is the peripheral nervous system? (PNS)

The human peripheral nervous system plays an important role in transmitting information from various parts of the body outside the brain and spinal cord to the brain and sending signals from the brain to other parts of the body. It consists of the brain and spinal cord and ganglia. The peripheral nervous system includes neuromuscular junctions, cranial nerves, and spinal nerves. Each of these systems carries information to the central nervous system. The peripheral nervous system is divided into two sections. It is divided into Somatic Nervous System and Autonomic Nervous System.

What are the four main functions of the peripheral nervous system?

1. Controls involuntary bodily functions.

2. Controls motor movements.

3. Activates digestive movements.

4. Sends sensory information to the central nervous system.

Cranial nervous system:

Cranial nerves are 12 pairs of nerves that connect directly to the brain, 11 of which are part of your peripheral nervous system. These 11 nerves activate the skin on your head, face, and neck, the five senses of sight (sight), smell (smell), sound (hearing), taste (taste), touch (body) and enables etc.

The vagus nerve runs down and connects to all the major organs from your neck to your colon.

Spinal nerves:

These are 31 pairs of nerves that connect to your spine at the same level as each segmental bone (vertebrae) in your spine. All of the above nerves divide into smaller nerves that travel throughout your body. They eventually end up on the tips of a person's fingers and toes or under the surface of your skin.

Our brain is a composite of Brahma force, Soul, Mind, Water, Particles, Elements, Chemicals, Electricity, Brain

Waves, Brain Frequencies, Energy, Sensation, Heat. The parts of the brain change according to the mind, thoughts, physical illness, health, circulation, etc. That is brain parts, body parts, spinal cord movement Occurs and becomes of the mind force, suitable for action is manifested.

Chapter 9

Some more information about the brain:

1. A neuron or nerve cell in the brain is an electrically excitable cell. A neuron is a specialized cell that can transmit information to muscle or gland cells. The neuron cell body consists of axons and dendrites.

2. The brain reason for the unique properties of the structure and function of interconnected neurons.

3. Nerve cells have a nucleus and cytoplasm. The axon extends from the cell body and forms many small branches before the nerve ends. Dendrites grow from the neuron's cell body and receive messages from other neurons.

4. Your brain is constantly generating bursts of electrical activity. In fact, how groups of neurons in your brain communicate with each other when your brain generates these electrical impulses is called brain wave activity.

5. The brain keeps adding more membranes and the function keeps growing

6. How do photoreceptors work in the brain?

Basically, the process is simple and involves chemically converting electromagnetism into electrical energy in a series of cascades. The process is called phototransduction. When photons enter the eye and strike the retina, they are detected by photoreceptor cells in the outer segment and converted into chemical energy. Then, this chemical signal is converted into an electrical signal. Through a change in membrane potential at the inner segment and the signal is converted back into a chemical signal, electricity at the synaptic terminal is the universal language of the nervous system.

7. The final destination of sensory information is the cortex, the outer layer of the brain. It does most of the high-level processing.

Examples:

Perception,memory, language, and emotion.

1. The brainstem and limbic system serve many important functions.

8. Gray and white matter:

The gray and white matter of the brain and spinal cord work together to form the spinal cord. These pathways send nerve (neuron) signals from your brain to the rest of your body. The gray matter of the dorsal part of the spinal cord relays the sense of hearing, Memory, speech, touch and temperature, and pain, and ventral horns have motor and motor neurons. White matter is the tissue in the central nervous system (CNS) that relays the actions of gray matter to areas where it is needed. It is white because of myelin. White matter damage affects mobility. Together, these two carry out many important functions in the human body, sending messages to the spinal cord and brain. The brain has many other functions. Research on the brain continues today and forever. This text is to explain that the brain works in harmony with cosmic energy. The gray matter of the spinal cord is a sensory relay. These are related to their feelings.

Example:

Pain, touch, temperature, ventral horn motor contains motor neurons.

9. Glossary Neuron: Cells in your nervous system called nerve cells or neurons are specialized to transmit neurotransmitter messages. Do neurons use chemicals to communicate with each other? Yes, chemicals are used

10. Neurotransmitters are small molecules that transmit a signal from one neuron to another neuron.

11. Our brain has power (mind force). Thus it manifests as energy. Thus, consciousness exists, has energy, stores information, has memory, and has thoughts, electromagnetic energy, chemical-electrical interaction, thermodynamic energy, and quantum phenomena. And it is like a computer that integrates and controls thousands of functions, internal energy, external energy, and movement.

12. Is there fluid around the brain?

Cerebrospinal fluid (CSF) is a clear fluid that surrounds the brain and spinal cord. The brain is cushioned and protected by cerebrospinal fluid. This watery fluid is produced by specialized cells in 4 hollow spaces in the brain called ventricles.

(CSF) What is cerebrospinal fluid made of?

Abstract CSF is a clear colorless ultra filtrate of plasma with low protein content and few cells.

CSF is mainly produced by the choroid plexus but is also produced by the ependymal lining cells of the brain's ventricular system.

13. What are amino acids?

Amino acids are the building blocks of protein. Proteins are long chains of amino acids. There are thousands of different proteins in your body, each of which has an important job. There are twenty different types of amino acids. Each protein has its own set of amino acids. These perform different functions in the body.

14. What do amino acids do for the brain?

For the brain to function, the central nervous system (CNS) needs many amino acids found in protein foods. The brain uses amino acids such as tryptophan, tyrosine, histidine, and arginine to synthesize various neurotransmitters and neuromodulators (Betz et al., 1994).

15. How many amino acids are in the human brain?

Are there?

Only about half of the 20 amino acids required for brain development and function can be synthesized in the central nervous system (CNS). Especially (-NH2) acidic carboxyl group and (-COOH) organic R group. It contains small neutral and anionic amino acids that act as neurotransmitters. Also contains some amino acids.

The power of the mind is active with the help of the brain through the interaction of the elements and molecules which are the products of the Brahma power of cosmic consciousness. So, little is explained about the brain.

Chapter 10

Brain functions depend on these:

1. The brain is full of positively and negatively charged molecules called ions. A neuron is negatively charged. The sum of all the negative ions' charges is greater than that of the positive ions. The difference in electric charges over its surroundings is called the Membrane potential of the tissue. 2. Voltage is a relative measurement, and neuroscientists always use the outside of the cell as a 'ground' or reference point to measure the voltage across the membrane. For example, if the inside of the cell is 50

mV more negative than the outside of the cell, the voltage will show as –50 mV.

3. There are many different potentials in the brain. These are the resting state of ions, action potential, short potential, depolarization (decreasing) hyperpolarization (increasing) in these cases Voltage path (gated) ion channels open and close. Here the voltage inside and outside the cell membrane is millivolt (mV) negative and positive.

4. For a neuron at resting it has about -65 millivolt. That difference may decrease or increase. Too many positive or negative ions remain in the neuron for a short time depending on the resting state.When depolarization reaches a threshold of -55, voltage-gated sodium ion channels located in the membrane of the initial segment of the axon open, allowing more positive ions to enter the neuron. That moment sets off a chain reaction of firing in the neuron and depolarization in segments near the end of the axonal trap.

Action potentials occur in the brain when the membrane potential of cells housing rapidly rises and falls. This depolarization then causes nearby sites to depolarize similarly.

Example: Excited cells such as neurons, muscle cells, plant cells, etc., have action potentials in many types of animal cells. Pancreatic beta cells, endocrine cells, and some cells of the anterior pituitary gland are excitatory cells that are all functioning. Therefore, according to the mind, the cells of the body parts are determined to act accordingly.

5. Amino acids such as glycine, glutamate, and GABA each have their own type of receptors.

6. Their target organs such as neurons and muscles are glands and part of the electrochemical transmission.

7. Our eyes transmit information through the optic nerve to a station deep within the brain through a unique structure called the retina. It starts sorting and processing what are the highest inputs, and from there the information goes to the visual cortex.

8. Motor neurons innervate your blood vessels your intestines your heart your bladder and all sorts of things.

9. Photoreceptors Light-sensitive cells in the retina convert photons into electrical signals. The eye has a remarkable dynamic range.

10. Five Senses Sensory Neurons: Sensory neurons are found in receptors such as the eyes, ear, tongue, and skin and carry nerve impulses to the spinal cord and brain. When these nerve impulses reach the brain, they are transformed into sensations such as sight, taste, hearing, and touch. A chemical input comes from taste or smell, which neurons send to the brain.

11. The thalamus transmits sensory impulses from receptors in various parts of the body to the cerebral cortex. A

sensory stimulus travels from the body surface to the thalamus, where it is received as a sensation.

12. Motor neurons are cells in the brain and spinal cord that send commands from the brain to the muscles that function, allowing us to swallow food, speak, and breathe.

13. LNG The lateral geniculate nucleus is located in the gross lateral part of the thalamus, located between the cortex and the midbrain.

The lateral geniculate nucleus belongs to the category of sensory protective nuclei of the thalamus and plays an important role in normal visual processing. In humans, both LNGs contain six layers of neuronal gray matter that alternate with the white matter of optic fibers. The LNG receives several strong feedback connections from the primary visual cortex.

14. The brain works with the help of the mind. The mind does not work with the help of the brain.

15. We associate mind and brain with intelligence because we use our brains to learn new facts and make decisions.

16. As many thoughts as you create in the brain, the mind force will be generated accordingly. For each thought, the neurons in the brain cause appropriate electrical signals. The endocrine glands of the brain, the organs of the brain, and the organs of the body produce various chemicals to suit each individual thought activity of the human being. Each of these chemicals has the potential for each

characteristic. A particular chemical product also has a particular philosophical nature. There are molecules for this. Those molecules are based on unique properties, vibrations, waves, interactions, and electricity. Therefore, when thoughts occur, when the chemical substance expresses its action, the human power for it is revealed, and then the electric energy that emerges from the brain through neurons becomes mind impulse and takes the form of time, cause, and action.

There are two types of synapses in the brain.

1. Electrical synapses.

2. Chemical synapses

These synapses convert the chemical signal back into electricity.

According to Peter Jedlicka, two theories of the impact of quantum phenomena on the brain:

Recent research has led to the existence of trivial quantum effects in biological systems. Although ana interactions with noisy and hot spin, they are sometimes due to it and because the brain is a complex non-linear system that is highly sensitive to small fluctuations, it can amplify microscopic quantum effects. In particular, there are two alternative but interrelated ways in which quantum phenomena can affect brain activity.

One, trivial quantum effects can scale up processes in living organisms at the micro scale, and two, nonlinear chaotic dynamics can amplify small-scale quantum fluctuations upward to modulate large-scale mesoscopic and macroscopic neural activity.

Revisiting the quantum brain hypothesis: towards quantum (neuro) biology? A full research explanation of this can be found at - Peter Jedlicka frontiersin.org

Chapter 11

What is a neuron?

Brain cells called neurons send information and instructions to all parts of the brain and body. Information is transmitted by electrochemical signals called action potentials that travel down the length of the neuron. The neurons are then stimulated to release chemical ions called neurotransmitters. They stimulate the action potentials of nearby cells. They help the signal spread throughout the body. A motor neuron is approximately 0.1 millimeters in diameter.

Chapter 12

What are Neurotransmitters?

Neurotransmitters carry chemical signals i.e. messages from one neuron to another nerve cell to the next destination. Neurotransmitters are chemical messengers without which your body cannot function. That important job is to carry chemical signals (messages) from one neuron to the next target cell. The next target cell may be another nerve cell, a muscle cell, or even a gland. These neurotransmitters control all of your nervous system movements, your thought processes, and your muscle and organ activity. Your nerve cells send and receive information from all body sources.

Chapter 13

Action potential:

Brain activity is how your brain sends impulses through the nerves (neurons) to move the arms. and send electrical impulses to many muscles in your arm. This allows you to move your hand properly. This action is the performance of the brain.

When we smell an, the olfactory neurons in the nose are capable of firing in response. The electrical activity ranges from -70mV to +40mV. Repolarization is -40mV to -70mV. The signal ends when the action potential is carried to the action terminal.

Chapter 14

Resting potential:

A neuron's membrane potential is the resting potential when it is not sending any impulses. The resting membrane potential in the brain means that there are more positively charged sodium ions outside the neuron than inside the cell. Likewise, more potassium ions are inside the neuron than outside. At this precise time, potassium channels are open. Sodium and chloride channels remain closed. The voltage is not neutral when the cell is at rest. But it can be said that there is voltage. Here the potential of electrical energy is measured inside and outside the membrane and there is a voltage which is called membrane potential. This voltage is minus 70 millivolts (-70Mv).

Diffusion

Electrostatic force

A charged particle is an ion.

Chapter 15

Receptor potential:

An example of a receptor potential is in a taste bud. There the taste is converted into an electrical signal that is sent to the brain.

It helps to regulate the electrolyte balance in the human body. Sodium is a very important resource for maintaining the proper functioning of neurons and muscles. Potassium is an important mineral that your body needs to function properly. It helps in regulating nerves and muscle contraction.

Ions contribute significantly to the resting tissue potential of cells. Extracellular potassium concentration is therefore an important regulator of cell excitability. Potassium ions help maintains cell osmolarity. Potassium is important for heart function and muscle and bone breakdown. Sodium and potassium maintain the body's electrolyte balance. Sodium ions are found in human cells such as nerve cells. It also regulates the flow of water throughout the tissue.

The function of the sodium-potassium pump in the brain is to pump sodium and potassium ions up and down the concentration gradient. Sodium ions are expelled and potassium enters.

This event is great work in the brain. Brain movement becomes important in the proper functioning of biological functions. Sodium potassium ions are very important for the transmission of nerve impulses in the human body. Sodium is needed to transport sugars and amino acids in cells. Potassium ions are found in cells. Potassium has a chemical connection to the brain.

Calcium ions contribute to the body and biochemistry of living organisms. They play an important role in signal transduction pathways from neurons to neurons and all muscle cell types participate in contraction and contraction. It also mediates calcium channels and organelles involved in heart and muscle contractions, transmission of neural information, learning, and memory.

It would take several books to cover the entire biological functions of the brain. So this explanation is just to know a little bit.

Chapter 16

Knowing about fundamental particles, atoms, and five forces can understand cosmic consciousness.

Basic Particles:

Due to the combination of light and sound energy, which was inherent in the origin of the universe, very fine and powerful energy was thrown into the atmosphere as a huge explosion in the space of light. Then as it expanded and cooled, the fundamental forces, the fundamental particles, were formed. These elementary particles are found in each period with different energies and properties. We may mention here a few, especially elementary particles. They are quarks, leptons, hadrons, neutrons, neutrinos, positrons, muons, tau baryons, mesons, photons, bonons, gluons, mosons, electrons, bosons, and some antiparticles. The basic elementary particles are still being discovered. Elementary particles are indivisible. It is this fundamental particle that evolves into an atom.

Chapter 17

What is an atom?

Atom refers to the smallest microscopic particle contained in a substance. The smallest particle of an element.

An atom has a positively charged nucleus at its center. Inside the nucleus are protons and neutrons, the neutrons are uncharged, and the electrons surrounding them are negatively charged. Atoms are the material elements of the universe, the building blocks of living things. Atoms contain light and intrinsic energy. Even today it remains untouched or without getting caught in the end. Each atom naturally has a positive and negative charge. Externally, the two types of charge create an electric force when the proton and neutron interact with the electron.

And each is its opposite.

Many texts must be written to know what the atom was created in ancient times. However, the above description of the atom will suffice for now.

Chapter 18

What is an element?

An element is any pure substance that cannot be separated further by physical or chemical methods. It is made up of the same type of atoms, not compound atoms.

Example;

If we take the element gold, it will contain only gold atoms.

There are 118 elements in total. 92 of these elements exist in nature. The remaining 26 elements are produced synthetically in laboratories. The names of 118 elements can be found in the table of elements.

Don't think that the elements exist only in some cosmic space. We have elements in our bodies.

Chapter 19

What is the atomic number?

The atomic number of an atom is defined as the number of protons in the nucleus or the number of electrons orbiting the nucleus of the element.

Each element has a different number of protons and electrons.

The first of these is the hydrogen atom. Its atomic number is 1.

A hydrogen atom has one proton and one electron. It is basically atomic number 1

Other elements have atomic numbers up to 2,3,4,5.....118.

The atomic number is denoted by the symbol z.

Chapter 20

Thirumoolar comments on the atom.

He says that an atom is a microscopic substance that is like an extended braid. The Higgs boson (God particle) looks like an extended braid. He says that the atom can be separated and has excellent energy. Moreover, the atom can be interpreted as light and sound, and the atom cannot be destroyed. If we divide the atom, the final form is the Lord and the Life (Siva) (Soul). He says that no one has fully seen the origin and cause of the atom. All these theories said by Thirumoolar agree with modern atomic scientists' views. Hundreds of scientists in various periods have expressed atomic theories with the help of modern and sophisticated instruments. No real scientist can deny this.

Thus, Thirumoolar was an amazing man. Atoms have been studied from ancient times to modern times. Especially ancient Indian and Greek philosophers commented on the atoms. There are references to it in many texts about the atom from very ancient times in India. Indian (Bharat)Philosophers Kanada. Thirumoolar and many other yogis have explained the principles of the atom. Today's science explains the properties of the particle very clearly. Research on the atom is a series of stories. The best scientists of modern times present their discoveries to the world.

Chapter 21

The basic force can be divided into five:

1. Universal Mind force
2. Gravitational force
3. Electromagnetic force
4. Strong nuclear force
5. Weak nuclear force

1. Universal Mind Force:

The Divine Consciousness or Cosmic Mind is the Brahma mind force that arose from it. From the intellect of the universe arose the power of the Brahma mind. Brahma mind force is a micro-power that manifests through prana, the moving force of the intellect. The Brahma Mana force is associated with subtle vibrational energy and unified field theory. The universal Brahma mind force is the absolute cause of all creations and forces in the universe. God or the creative cosmic consciousness creates itself as vibrations and becomes the cosmic image of dependent illusion as Kala, Karya, Karana, Lord.

From the most subtle Brahma mind force, the mind force of humans and other living beings is formed. Like other basic keys, this key is very subtle. Man has achieved various achievements by using this mind force properly. Immeasurable energy is thus manifested. In the Universal Brahma mind, each part of your body has its own memory. Likewise, the cells, chromosomes, DNA, and RNA (Gene) in your body remember the characteristics. Especially the heart, lungs, brain, liver, spleen, kidney, uterus, stomach, etc. do not always change from their movement characteristics. Your body is the soul, mental body, cell body, food body, fleshy body, and chemical body, and these can be thought of as a sense of accepting the six types of actions.

2. Gravity:

Gravitational force is the force that attracts two objects to each other—this gravitational force acts throughout the universe. The fundamental particles and atoms in the universe are each other attracts. The force of gravity on the earth is equal to the force the earth exerts on you. The force of gravity on the Earth's surface equals your weight. So all particles have gravitational force acting on them depending on their respective mass or energy.This gravitational force varies depending on the mass and nature of each of the planets, stars, milky way, galaxies, and other cosmic objects.

As far as the Earth is concerned, it pulls on objects within it and objects approaching from space. This force works in the solar system, the milky way, and other universes. Gravity also pulls light. A black hole is the densest gravitational force in the universe. Even light cannot escape this gravity. Gravitational force or gravitation is essential for the earth. Without this force, we would be flying in space instead of on Earth. There is no way that we and other terrestrial creatures could have come into being. This gravitational force keeps us and other material objects attached to the Earth. This gravity preserves our Earth's weather conditions by preventing the atmosphere from disintegrating and drifting off into the vast expanse of space. This is also an important reason for maintaining habitable conditions on Earth. And how does Earth's gravity work? Bosons carry messages between atoms in our bodies and other atoms that can be detected on Earth. These particles attract each other. Every object in the universe attracts each other. This force of gravity was clearly explained by a scientist named Newton. In this gravitation, the cosmic creative things are united in diversity. These include mass, weight, light, speed, momentum, gas, elementary particles, distance, density force reaction of gravity, inertia, space of the universe, time, energy, a life of matter, etc.

Dark energy may be the connection between living things, dark matter, and other things such as gravity or gravitation force but we are unknown of it.

3. Electromagnetic force:

The electromagnetic force is the interaction between electrically charged particles. Protons are present in the nucleus of atoms. At their core is the interaction of bosons called photons, which is the electromagnetic force. This interaction is exchanged between the protons and nearby electrons and the electrons in the nucleus. Electrons move around the nucleus by electromagnetic force. The electric field acting on the electromagnetic field and the magnetic field are coupled to each other.

Electromagnetic force acts between charged particles. It is related to magnetism and electricity. Light is an electromagnetic wave. Light is a quantum of the electromagnetic field. Magnetic forces and electric forces are the same kind of fundamental force. James Clark Max Wellin, a physicist, in 1873 in describing an essay on electromagnetism. This was later confirmed. Until then, the electromagnetic force was considered to be separate. Light, heat, and microwaves are emitted as waves in the universe. All these together can be called electromagnetic radiation.

4. Strong nuclear force:

The strong nuclear force is the force that causes the formation of a stable nucleus that contains all the particles in the nucleus. This force causes the nuclei of atoms to come together at a certain distance rather than moving apart. Specifically, the nucleus of an atom is composed of two elements. It contains protons and neutrons. These have the property of being unchanging. So protons are always particles with positive currents. Thus the protons become repulsion to each other as they have similar electric charges. Here the force of exclusion comes into play. Nature does her work very well in this regard. This repulsive force causes the protons to move away from each other. But they undergo strong nuclear processing so they can't get away. This is the strong nuclear force. This means that a stable nucleus of very small microscopic size cannot contain more than one proton without neutrons.By reducing the repulsive force between the positively charged proton particles in the neutron particle nucleus, a strong force involving all the particles in the nucleus results in the formation of a stable nucleus. This strong force is called the strong nuclear force.

Weakest nuclear force:

As the number of protons increases in the nucleus, the repulsive force does not act, and the nuclei of some elements spontaneously disintegrate or break into smaller particles, radiating energy. The force responsible for this radioactive decay is the weak nuclear force. This energy also plays an important role in the formation of stars in space. This force also acts on unstable atoms, nuclear fusion, and the reactive motion of atoms. The weak nuclear force is essentially radioactivity.

Chapter 22

What is Akasa?

Akasa is a term that refers to the entire space that we see and call the universe. This sky has a grandeur that cannot be described by words. It was that the sky and the cosmic consciousness or Parabrahma had never arisen. Therefore, it means that the cause is not created.

As you travel through space, space continues to limitless expand. The material found throughout the universe originated from the original material called the sky. Gravitational force, electromagnetic force, atomic force, binding force Explanation All forces and life forces originate from one force called Prana. The power of Prana in the sky is called Ceprapancham and all its objects are made of the same substance according to Hindu philosophers and they call it Akasa. Everything that we human beings and other creatures in other universes see, feel, touch and taste are different manifestations of the mental force of this space i.e. the Brahma mind force. Subtle forces in the universe, mind, thought, elementary particles, atoms, solid, liquid, gas, form, body, earth, sun, moon, stars, and many other universes are all made of Akasa. A very subtle energy called prana is the source of the aerial forces. It is an indisputable fact that by its power all the above phenomena come into motion, exist, and perish. It is a matter of great to the human that the Indian yogis knew this universality or essential by intuition long ago.

Chapter 23

An explanation according to the science of prana?

Prana, in short, is the most subtle energy that operates in the infinite universe or universe, the Brahma mind force of Moola Prakriti, Suksuma, and material objects. The nature of the universe is made up of two types of matter. One of them is Akasa and the other is Prana. Akasa is dependent on material objects.Prana is the energy that transforms space into many forms. That is, the rishis assert that it is this Prana that gives a power or energy to make everything in the universe, from material things to living matter, function as time, matter, and cause. This very subtle energy called prana is responsible for the functioning of the human mind and body. In another way, prana can also mean life force. As far as we are concerned with this book, we can stop with the fact that mental energy requires prana. But life is not a substance made of space or prana.It is immaterial. So it is eternal and at the same time, the subtle body which is the source of the transformation of prana into a subtle form of thought is also made from the subtle form of Akasa.The natural fundamental forces of the universe, whether gravity, attraction, repulsion, heat, electricity, or magnetism, are all one. Although these differ, they are not mutually exclusive. Living things, human beings, and aliens, whether they are the thoughts of the mind arising from the causes of their internal organs or the actions arising from the external organs, are all. They are based on the energetic subtle energy called prana by Indian sages.

Prana is vibration, a kind of vibration.

Yaditham kinja jagat sarvam prana ejati ni:srutam - Sanskrit

Explanation: It is said that everything in this universe comes into being due to the vibration of Prana.

Prana is a form of energy. What is it?

From a yogic perspective, prana is the primordial energy of the universe. Prana is dispersed throughout the physical world. Prana is macrocosmic and microcosmic and is the source of all life. Our body is red, prana is green and the mind is blue. Sri Aurobindo mentions colors like blue, green, and red as follows. They represent the mind, prana, and the physical body respectively. Similarly, the green screen which is the Vallalar rathi means spiritual desires, especially prana, "my form of transformation" (for the transformation of the physical body) The red color also represents the physical body as the Lord has a golden form appears and gives a red color flower. The soul consists of the inner mind, inner prana, and inner body. The inner mind is golden blue or golden yellow, the inner prana is golden green or purple, and the inner body is golden red. its purest inner body is golden in color.

A white screen covers the soul's most recently pure consciousness and increased sub consciousness, so the purest inner mind or mature intellect appears white, or white mixed with yellow, and generally the inner psycho-prana-body philosophies appear white.

Inside the center of the eyebrow hangs a flesh that is white at the bottom and yellow at the top. Sri Aurobindo explains that intellect appears as yellow, the mind as blue, and prana as green or purple. The golden screen and the white veil are close to the soul in the depths of the inner mind. The internal prana in your mind activates the internal bodywork. Therefore, such internal prana should be considered as the green color of Ponmayi, which Vallalar says. I can imagine that the inner prana appears as a green screen to the gold as the senses descend from the golden paraparaveli(universe) into the inner prana. Sri Aurobindo mentions in Savitri Kavya that there are three powers that are closest to the soul in the depths of the inner mind, one power in dim color and then another soul power in golden purple light, and still deeper there is a soul power in pure light.

Through inner purity, kindness, devotion, love, and meditation, he goes to your face and in concentrated mental energy, in its position, with the intense desire to seek the Lord, crosses the sixth screen and his life sees his own soul, the true soul. This true form (meipathy) is white in color. The inner states of the soul, the inner mind, the inner prana, and the inner body are understood to have each color.

Chapter 24

The six basic elements of nature: their qualities and function, are described here.

1. Universal Mind.
2. Akasam (space)(ether)
3. Air.
4. Fire
5. Water.
6. Land.

World's primary concept – C.Poongavanam

Six basic elements are different from each other.

But creativity is found in unity. However, these have karu(basic energy) characteristics. They are mind(creator), sabda (sound), touch (sparsa), rupa (form), and rasa(taste), gandham (smell) and which are the six properties. The creation of the mind's energy is space, sound in space, and sound in air, and both are equivalent. Fire has the three qualities of sound, touch, and form. Water has four qualities of sound, touch, form, and rasam, and earth has five qualities of sound, touch, form, rasam, and gandham. Through these elements, creation and its other powers are intertwined and come into motion. In India, the mind Since ancient times clear theories about.

Chapter 25

Paramahamsa Yogananda said about the mind:

October 16, 1938, First Self-Realization Fellowship Temple, Encinitas, California.

The universe has all the forces or vibrations. The vibration of speech and thoughts is so that they are external appearances. Human thoughts of all vibrated. The vibration rate of the thoughts wave is too high. Its hasn't been found yet.

Hypothetical space is assumed not to be necessary to explain a scientific theory about the nature of the planet. But the Hindu shastras have a subtle vibration in the sky or space. Creations are placed on it. It is the vibration energy that fills all the interstices of space and separates all forms from one another. If you are very close and in love with someone you can sense their thoughts. This is impossible unless you fix your boundaries. Those who practice concentration and meditation regularly in your Self-Relationship Fellowship (Yogatha Satsang Society) hymns and who are very quiet can perceive the thoughts of others even from afar. Your mind becomes more sensitive.

We are all human radios and you receive the messages of others through your heart, the center of your consciousness. The highest level of intuition is the spinal cord, where your consciousness transmitting and receiving apparatus is. Suppose you are away from home and you want to know what is going on there. If your emotions are calm and your mind calm, you will be able to intuit the feelings and thoughts of your family at home. When you develop the power of great mental integration your consciousness can penetrate everywhere and your perception becomes saturated with energy and electricity.

This world is a thought in God's mind.

Therefore, it is God's mental force that created the stars and all the worlds and the mind is the main factor that holds together the living cells of our body in which creation is fully functioning. The wonderful state of consciousness in every particle of matter is the complete work of that divine mind which needs no equipment to accomplish its purpose.

The energy of our small minds is part of the Lord's powerful mental energy. Below our consciousness is the infinite great ocean of His consciousness. Today's science suggests that vibration is the main mechanism behind human consciousness. Scientists say that thoughts are vibrations.

Chapter 26

What is the human mind?

A. Definition of Mind? (manas)

Mind is a force. It is united with the power of the Brahma mind and manifests in living beings with the help of the soul. Other senses depend on their input.

Brahma mind force is connected to the mind or manas, intellect(buddhi), ego(ahankara), Chitta, and the living body (atma) (feelings) acting in harmony with it. This mind is exceptionally capable of moving the mind without the body by the power of a pure Yogi.

Generally in Bharat (India), Andakaranas mean manas, intellect, ego, and chitta. These four constitute the body, the nose, the eye, the ear, the mouth, and the five senses, i.e. sight, touch, smell, hearing, and taste. Thoughts, feelings, nature, matter, cause and karya (action) memory, forgetfulness, wakefulness, dream, sleep, Illusion, Intuition, Benevolence, Evil, Karma, Enlightenment, Awareness, Subconsciousness, Superconsciousness, Superhigher consciousness, Chemical Changes, Basic Forces, Energies, Brahma force, Samadhi, Mukti depend on these total factors. It will have its impact or manifestation depending on the respective events.

In India, the mind is divided into four types namely Buddhi, Mind, Agankaram Siddha. The mind is also aware of the many natural things in the universe. The mind is engaged and attached to them. Then it is the mind to be clear and doubt about whether it is this or that. The mind is the instrument that integrates the five senses, the brain, and the information and expresses the sensations in less than a second of the moment. Thus, there are eight-dimensional memories in the mind. They are basic memories, atomic memories, genetic memories, evolutionary memories, karmic memories (past birth), clear and vague memories, and conscious and unconscious memories. Some of the pre-born connections in the mind are born naturally without being taught.

No matter how many births the mind takes, it does not change i.e. it does not lose that unique quality. All thoughts and actions after death are included in life. Life is experienced and embodied in the soul.

When the soul takes birth again, the soul which is in the middle of the eyebrows becomes life in the continent, and then in karanas the whole body becomes alive and active. Experiences gained in previous births are also knowledge follows. That is why some people have past birth memories.

This primordial mind is transmitted from birth to birth naturally and the sages attain the benefit of many births. Even ordinary people are gifted in certain activities.

The mind is composed of three layers. The first in this layer is made up of thoughts. This is the first superficial layer. Next to this, the second layer is made up of emotions. This layer is slightly deeper than the previous one.But not deep enough. The third layer is the most important. This layer represents the silence.A state without sounds, thoughts, and feelings. The first layer is related to the head, i.e. the brain. The second layer is based on the heart. The third layer is our subconscious state.- Osho.

B. What is (Buddhi)?(intellect)

Intellect means to know something by inquiry. In other words, intelligence is the tool for knowing and clarifying the name, race, quality, and profession of an object. Knowledge is generated through intellect. The intellectual process is commonly referred to as the mind. It is called Buddhi. It basically works from limited data. It has collected mostly conscious data. Sometimes it accesses data. But mostly it works only from conscious data.

Intellect and knowledge are interrelated, but what is the difference between intelligence and knowledge?

The intellect is selfish and desires to achieve whatever the intellect desires. Evil can be done.
Knowledge transcends desires and sees truth and eternal life. It is for the common good. This is the knowledge that waits for good from evil.
If the mind listens to the words of knowledge, the mind listens to the words of wisdom, and the senses listen to the words of the mind, it is the action of knowledge. That is soul knowledge. If it works without the support of knowledge, it is Jiva knowledge. If everything else works without the means of the intellect, it is the work of the mind and that is mental knowledge. Knowledge is the retention of what is gained from all that can be seen in this universe. It adjusts to suit each individual mind.Its expansion will be based on each individual ability. Knowledge is the ability of man to impart good and bad effects according to the way in which he chooses to use it.
In the Universal Mind, everything is already united in it. As man knows it and goes inward, the Universal Mind reveals it to the mind through individual knowledge. So nothing is new to the universe. It is new to man. This is where the mind force comes action into play and brings them.

C. What is Ego(Ahankara)?
Egoism is the feeling of being an individual self and wanting to achieve something in life. It can function depending on his senses. There is selfishness in it. So will public interest. It activates one's actions, so one should be present with modesty. It is your identity.

the theory that egoism is what every being is herself. It refers to his body as I. An arrogant sense of self comes to the fore.

Reality is the loss of self-personality (the ego). Destroy the ego by searching for its identity. Because the (ego) self is not a subjective entity. Self-disappearing and self-revealing reality. - Ramana Maharishi.

See who has this doubt. Who is the doubter? Who is the thinker? That is the ego. Hold this. Other thoughts will perish. The ego is purified; See where the ego arises from. That is pure consciousness.-Ramana Maharishi.

E. What is Chitta? (chittham)

Chitta is a determination to achieve something.
Chitta is the subconscious state of the individual or the state of pure awareness and attaining the state of cosmic consciousness that is great to know. It attains pure bodily light. Mind, intellect, and ego travel on a separate path which is the ultimate limit of Siddha. The full benefit of Siddha is achieved by the higher beings who have attained pure body, and pure karanas (96 philosophy) such as Siddhas, spiritual sages, yogis, rishis, etc. Exceptionally few return to cosmic consciousness. This Sid cosmic state of consciousness can only be known by the Incomparable Jivan. Those who reached this stage were called Siddhas in Tamil. It has the total attributes of mind, intellect, ego, and integrated and universal consciousness. Through meditation, one can touch the full evolutionary and dimensional boundaries of the will. When the clarity of will becomes pure, your physical vibrational connection

becomes one with the cosmic vibration. When you feel oneness with nature, you are in a state of cosmic consciousness at will.

Mind has five levels. It is waking, dream, sleep, duriya and duriyaditham.

In general, modern scientists and ancient philosophers who study the mind, medieval and modern philosophers and philosophers of mind are focused on examining the things that appear to the senses. They examine only things that are palpable to the senses and the mind. Scientists analyze what reaches their senses in parts and do many experiments and say its philosophy. According to them mind is waking, dreaming, and sleeping, leaving these three states of mind they can never carry out research beyond this. But there are two other states beyond these waking, dream, and sleep.

Indian yogic philosophy refers to the states of mind as Duryam and Duryadhitam. None but the best Yogis can know these high qualities of the above two states of mind. Here, the subject of our book, mind force, operates in these five stages. Indian yogic philosophy refers to the states of mind as it is called Duryam and Duryadhitam.

They perceive this from the universe, i.e. through the Brahma force, through waking, dreaming, sleeping, Durya, Duryadhitam. Both duriyam and duriyaditham can be realized through inner awareness.

Thurium is self-forgetfulness. It means the state where the mind is awake in the sleep of knowledge (mental power). Duryam is the state in which a soul perceives its state. When the meditative mind is connected with the prana, the mind reaches the state of Duryam consciousness, only the consciousness of the soul becomes apparent. In this state, there is no sense of the nature of the body. There is a very subtle movement of prana inside as the breath is held. When a soul reaches the Durya state, that individual's brain has theta waves. At that time its frequency is 4-8 Hz. In the state of Duryaditham, when the pure mind rests in the soul, then there is no soul-consciousness. It is that which itself shines forth (tattvamasi, you are that). In this state, the breath stops and the prana, the mind, the mind, and the Brahma force remain in the soul. When a soul reaches the Duryadhitham state, the brain of that individual has delta waves (brain waves). At that time its frequency is 0.5 Hz.

Thirumoolar Thirumantram Song 2159.

Explain:

It is within the chakra of consciousness that the state of bliss is established. When this stage is reached, the five Gnanendriyas, the five Kanmendriyas and the four anthakaranangal become 14 foxes and die. The horse then sped away. and now the soul has left the state of Durya and reached the blissful state of Duryathidam. Words cannot express the joy of receiving it.

- Thirumoolar Thirumantra Hymn 2863.

Explain:

Inactivity i.e. Duriya, unconsciousness i.e. ego mind is a state of condensation that cannot be explained in words. If the mind is subsumed in that unattainable state of discipline, then the mind will remain in a state where there is neither wakefulness nor sleep. In this state, his image will disappear and his thoughts about his body will disappear completely. Thirumoolar says that this is a blissful experiential condition.

Swami Vivekananda said about knowledge:

Knowledge means knowing something as distinct from ourselves. For example, we may think something but bring it out of the mind and distinguish it from the mind. Everything I see and know is in our minds. It is in the mind as samskaras as images. The first work of knowledge is to bring them out when we try to think about them. Knowledge is something inherent in humans. No knowledge comes from outside of man but inside within him. It should be said that a man discovers or removing back the screen in proper psychological language. As such, it means that man learns and discovers, in reality, an infinite mine of knowledge, removing back the curtain that covers his soul. We say that Newton discovered gravity. It was not waiting for him in a corner. It was in his mind and the moment came he discovered it. Indeed, all the knowledge that human society has ever acquired in the world has come from the mind. The infinite library in the universe is within your mind. The outer world is just a trigger for you to explore your mind, it is only an opportunity. But the object you are going to explore is also your mind. The apple falling from the tree was an inspiration for Newton. He searched his mind through it. So when he systematized all the of thoughts from his mind he discovered a new connection between them. We call it the law of gravity. This rule does not exist at Apple or Earth Center.

All material knowledge or spiritual knowledge is in the mind. In many people, these are closed without being discovered. We are said to be learning when the blinding screens are slowly removed. The amount of knowledge we get depends on the extent to which this screen is removed. The one from whom this screen is removed is the most knowledgeable person, the one from whom this screen is heavy, he is ignorant. someone who opens the mind screen he knows all things. Today there are still omniscient. I believe there will be in the future as well. They will appear in millions in the ages to come. The reasoning is superior to feelings. Better than this reasoning is intuition. Better than this intuition is enlightenment. Higher than wisdom is the attainment of the mind of Brahma (Barapbrahmam).

Thus, according to Vivekananda's ideas, my ideas, when any man connects his mind with the Brahman force and tries to use his search as a trigger, the universe gives the result by explaining the answer, i.e. what is hidden behind the veil.

Consciousness is the raw knowledge, the individual human soul, the most subtle, conscious, most conscious mind. Depending on the prana connection, each individual has subtle sensations and feelings, natures, in nature, with differences that manifest as the force of the mind. His understanding of an object, attention, hearing, mental integrity, better brain, better senses, better memory, religion, awareness, thinking ability, one action, experiences of previous birth, true knowledge of ancestors, best books, its relevance in the present day, civilization,Education,Knowledge,Philosophy, Spin and earth's topography, Economy of a country, Scientific development, Community mentality, Individual's likes and dislikes, Wealth level discrimination, Physical sensations and affect, Vision, Modern scientific instruments, Subconscious mind, Consciousness, Super Consciousness emerges depending on these. Other organisms exhibit knowledge at their evolutionary rate. Alien intelligence is also based on the evolution of their brains.

This is the intellect which is called Sidh. The basis of consciousness is Purusha which means the soul. Being the cause of everything we call knowledge.

Sadhguru's statement:

Chitta is the living mind. It is the intelligence of the Creator that works in every cell of our body. it is Chitta. Chitta is the intellect that transcends all old impressions and egoism. If you associate with it, God will be your slave. The Chitta is a mind without memory—pure intelligence. This intelligence is like cosmic intelligence. Simply exists. That is why everything happens. It doesn't work out of memory it simply works. What you call the universe is a living mind. Whether you are awake or asleep the will is always Chiita in motion and your intellect comes and goes and many times it fails even when you are awake. You can't be alive if you don't always have the Chitta or intelligence inside you Try to control your breath with your intelligence and you'll go crazy. Will is what keeps you alive and keeps you going. It's about touching the dimension of your mind. --.

It becomes your Chitta (Chiittame). If you want to attain the state of divine experience (divine rapture) called Sidh, you must attain the corresponding principles. After attaining these principles, the status of the individual is elevated to the position of the one who is the sustainer of the universe, who knows the movement of every atom of the universe, and the soul of everyone, who is the source of intelligence of this universe. Our forefathers bear witness to this.

Zenguru makes a very simple point about the mind.

That is, to a Zen master

One said: The flag is waving.

Another recounts the same incident:

The wind is blowing.

The Zen Guru, listening patiently, narrates this phenomenon in his own beautiful style.

He says not the vine, not the wind, the mind is moving.

So the power of the mind depends on the existence of the universe. It comes into motion only with the help of five mindless goblins. By seeing, hearing, feeling, knowing, knowing, and trying to know, the mind grasps and motions the universe.

The mind functions with the help of the five basic elements and the five senses. If there is damage to the human brain, if there is a disability in the human body, the proper development of the brain will be hindered so that the human mind does not function properly.

Mind is the name given to the aggregate of states of consciousness grouped under thinking, willing, and feeling. - Blavatsky says so in The Secret Doctrine.

Future mind or mental force:

Prana Consciousness and Mental Consciousness come down to the body from above and remain on the earth. This is the current state of mind evolution. But in the future, he explains that in the future, the luminous senses of the upper mind, the light mind, the higher mind, and the higher mind(Athi mind), one after the other, will come down into the man and prepare him to bear the thuula consciousness, after that the scientific consciousness with golden light will come down into the man and the body will turn into a golden body and attain immortality. - Sri Aurobindo's book Savitri is the secret of wisdom.

When a person reaches the above four types of mental state, his feelings will be higher than the current state. Then the power of the human mental force will reach a more powerful evolutionary stage than the mind force of the evolved human before. When man attains this stage man possesses the best civilized qualities. A man deals with the feelings of others very carefully. The tribulations of man as he is today are unlikely to exist then. Man's way of life is unlikely to correlate to today's situation. A different kind of economy would be better for humans in the future. His thoughts will be at a very high level. Often he will have reached a stage of evolution where humans can perform certain actions through his mind, i.e. a renaissance stage that he has never seen before in the history of human life. Some humans will also have the ability to transform their body into a light body(light). Some people may not be able to become the light body (light) of their condition. So here we need to know one thing, it is clear that man can make the atoms work according to his thought i.e. by his mind as the highest level of dimensional and dimensional development. He will have a combination of pure mind force energy, physical energy, and the energy to drive spaceships, which can make long-distance travel in space very easy. The power of meditation will give a hand to the future man. Atma, Mana, Prana, and Sukkuma Dekas are all mature to achieve immortality.

In the future, man's mind force will be used to create artificial intelligence (autonomous computer-aided thinking tools, i.e., robotics). It is modern artificial intelligence machine tools, human machines called robotics which perform many types of tasks for humans that a normal human can do. Artificial Intelligence is helping us in many ways today.

Mottos in Bharat(India) about the human mind:

1. He who is Chitta deranged will become mad.
2. No knowledge? He has no brain.
3. There is only a brain stem. No brain for him.

So, he will be in a state where his mind, intellect, and ego are disturbed. He will be unstable. He will be insensitive. It means he will not be conscious.

Chitta is another name for the cause of mind, intellect, and ego. Chittam is ideology. It is the mentality. Here is the state where all those factors are condensed.-Thayumanaver.

Chapter 27

What is Consciousness?

Consciousness is the mind, intellect, ego, Chitta, five traps, inner and outer phenomena and they are connected to each other. All these are related to the soul. Your consciousness is in the mode of dealing with natural and artificial (by your actions) dangers. A mosquito bites you. At that time the force of the mind will stimulate the senses and repel the mosquito. It is a natural risk. If you light a candle and the candle melts from the heat and hits your body, your senses will try to block the irritation caused by the heat. The hand will rush towards that place. This is a risk caused by your actions.

Here the force of mind activates sensation through your brain. Only you can know your sensation. Sensation is the nervous system module of the brain.

Consciousness is different. The thought is different. A thought comes from the force of the mind. But both contribute to the body with the help of the brain and are in touch with the soul. If the parts of the brain are affected due to any reason, then there is no feeling. The mind also does not work. All the senses of the mind act in the same way and its actions are subjective. It is only when the mind reacts that we know the object. In order to feel these, usually the parts of the brain and its associated organs and nerves, especially the spinal cord, sensory nerves, motor nerves, central nervous system (CNS), peripheral nervous system (PNS), and many other nerves are needed. From the time when the human being is formed in the embryo and the brain develops and then leaves the womb as a child until death, all the activities encountered are the contribution of emotion. There are many types of emotion. The appropriate response to the action is positive or negative.Waking, dreaming, sleeping, self-preservation, i.e. self-preservation, individual human characteristics, other living beings, characteristics, etc. Consciousness is related to the Brahma mind force (universe), soul, mind, body, brain, etc.

Every human being naturally has many emotional states. In the power of the human mind lies the potential for a higher consciousness beyond the limits of ordinary life. Through this higher consciousness, he can live a higher and wider life than he is now. Even an ordinary human being is by this higher order in his life. When a man's consciousness begins to occur, the mind forces vibration in action . The consciousness knows and does the unknowable and the unable actions. It is like a lamp burning in the center of man. Its light radiates through the dense coverings of his outer consciousness. It derives its truth and its power from life experiences. This nature and the consciousness of the Brahma force are being developed as a plan of superiority and norms in the system of individual life. Only a few individual souls are naturally capable of grasping the feelings of this truth through mental force. In this way, they help human society by using their life ability. Generally, man thinks in the thoughts of all human beings due to the force of mind and feels the vibrations of other people's senses and his vibrations. He plows in it. By his nature, the change of life by the power of the mind will remain in a balanced state of livelihood. No revival takes place in the human mind. We are conscious in this universe which includes three senses waking state, sleeping state, and dream state. Each living being's consciousness is unique. Generally, in the state of consciousness, each characteristic and corresponding change occurs in living beings. Humans, animals, birds, reptiles, aquatic life, plants, bacteria, viruses, and aliens have acquired this altered state of consciousness. In our body i.e. our waking state we are able to see what we can see through our senses. Consciousness is different for the senses for sleep and dream state the same sense acts on the senses in three ways.

The same feeling manifests itself in pure formlessness in pure yogis. Here this consciousness comes into action through the power of the mind. Yogis' mind power is differentiated by pure consciousness. Due to the power of the mind, the three types of activities namely waking, sleeping, and dreaming act differently on the human consciousness. It is because of the action of the senses that those feelings appear and remain in motion and disappear. Thus consciousness helps a man in movement with the power of the mind and helps other beings.

Spiritual Response

This is the intelligence called Sidh. The basis of consciousness is Purushane i.e. soul. Being the cause of everything we call knowledge.

Consciousness is what we experience with prajna, external and intuitive. It means intuition or Agaa consciousness.

Unconsciousness is unconscious unconsciousness.

It is the can't enjoy feeling at the bottom of our minds. - Osho

Every feeling is the result of a movement of thoughts with its content, and your feeling is the content of fear, hope, loneliness, anxiety, and sorrow. J. Krishnamurthy.

Chapter 28

What is the nature of consciousness?

Every human being naturally has many emotional states. In the power of the human mind lies the potential for a higher consciousness beyond the limits of ordinary life. Through this higher consciousness, he can live a higher and wider life than he is now. Even an ordinary human being is by this higher order in his life.When a man's consciousness begins to occur, the mind forces vibration in action. The consciousness knows and does the unknowable and the unable actions. It is like a lamp burning in the center of man. Its light radiates through the dense coverings of his outer consciousness. It derives its truth and its power from life experiences. This nature and the consciousness of the Brahma force are being developed as a plan of superiority and norms in the system of individual life. Only a few individual souls are naturally capable of grasping the feelings of this truth through mental force. In this way, they help human society by using their life ability. Generally, man thinks in the thoughts of all human beings due to the force of mind and feels the vibrations of other people's senses and his vibrations. He plows in it. By his nature, the change of life by the power of the mind will remain in a balanced state of livelihood. No revival takes place in the human mind.

From the time the human being is formed in the embryo and the brain develops, and then leaves the womb as a child to death, all the activities encountered are the contribution of emotion. There are many types of emotions. The response to the appropriate action is either positive or negative. we are waking, dreaming, sleeping, and trying self-preservation. Individual human traits are the traits of other living beings. These are mental in nature. Consciousness is related to the Brahma mental force (universe), soul, mind, body, brain, etc. The subconscious mind and intuition are also present in the mind. We will discuss this in the next section.

Spiritual Answer:

According to Karma, the senses of the individual are there. Due to the karma of previous births, it will be good or bad in this birth. It will act in their life.

It has no memory of before birth. It means silence, soul. Its limit, the end of consciousness, knows the soul.

Chapter 29

What is a thought?

The thoughts that appear in your mind.

Thoughts change from moment to moment. Man and living things have thoughts.

It is necessary for living organisms. Human thoughts are the main factor in actions and human creations. The reason for the great change in human society is the evolution of thought. The brain generates an average of 60,000 to 80,000 thoughts per day due to the force caused by the thoughts of the human mind. The brain generates at least 2500 to 3300 thoughts in an hour. The action of mind force on the thoughts of the mind is manifested depending on the causal basis of an individual's knowledge, culture, brain development, education, experience, individualistic attitude, nature of work, social customs, etc. The role of the five senses in developing thoughts is very important. It is due to the processing and understanding of these that thoughts arise and become sensations or are stimulated into sensations.

Atoms in the human body have certain natural properties. The impulses that occur according to your thoughts create different vibrations. Then the phonon and photon are attracted to the positively and negatively charged electrons corresponding to the energy. Small electrical currents occur in the human body due to chemical reactions according to the activities in the human body. Nerves, for example, transmit signals by conducting electrical impulses. Most biochemical reactions in the human body and all brain functions are driven by the recombination of charged particles. Also, chemical reactions in the human body emit small numbers of photons, elementary particles of light, in addition to releasing energy and producing heat. According to your thoughts, according to the force of the mind, different frequencies are released from the body without the eyes being aware of it.

Thus, our thought is the integration of a collection of various cosmic objects.

For example:

Spiritual consciousness is stimulated while reading spiritual texts. Philosophical feelings are stimulated while reading philosophical texts. Reading good books inspires positive interest and progressive actions. Your senses are easily stimulated by visuals. Your thoughts are stimulated by the words you hear.

Thoughts manifest in millions and millions of different people. You will find out about these in my next book.

Chapter 30

The power of thought comes from the universe:

Thought power comes from the thought essence of the universe, for good or evil. In manifesting creation, the Lord first manifests it in thought systems, the most subtle form of creation. Then they freeze into subtle forms of light and then into macroscopic atomic structures. If the original thought of God is removed, creation dissolves. Man's thoughts are borrowed in a subtle way from God's thinking power. Therefore they have the power to affect his own health, happiness, and success even when they are not developed. If they are reinforced by the same thoughts of others, they gain the power to influence the world in which they live. The thought systems implanted in creation by God are thus influenced either harmoniously or significantly uncongenially by the thoughts of mankind. - Paramahamsa Yogananda.

Thought is the primordial energy and vibration emanating from God, thus the creator of life, electrons, atoms, and all forms of energy. Thought is the greatest vibration energy, the fastest of all energies.- Paramahamsa Yogananda

Chapter 31

How does energy come into this mind?

Mind is a physical entity that derives its power for action from the cosmic Brahma mind force. The mind is a subtle manifestation. But powerful. The mind can appear alive and physical. It is the electric or liquid life (chemical life) and the solid gross body (cell body) mind invisible man or soul. Life or Prana is the liquid mind. and the body is solid. It is a simple theory about the mind. Human mental energy manifests as thoughts and feelings through the brain. Along with the soul, the force of the mind, thoughts, brain (chemical change), and feelings have come into action. A ship going to sea, natural power, and machinery, need only then the ship will come into motion. In this way, the mind's force requires knowledge, senses, karmendriya, gynanendriya. Also, the cranial nerves in the brain require the visual center. The power of thought has an effect even on those at a great distance. The old Sangya philosophers used two terms to refer to nature. One is the word Prakriti, which is very similar to the word nature, and the other is the scientific term Avyaktam. Avyaktam means that everything is without variation, atoms; molecules, energy, mind, thought, knowledge, etc. are the root cause of origin.

It's just that all knowledge and all power is within us and not outside. Energies are the secrets of nature and everything we say is the active force within. Existence in the external world is only change and there is no knowledge in nature. All knowledge comes from the human soul. He manifests and discovers within himself the knowledge that is eternally within him. Knowledge resides in the soul. It can be revealed when a favorable opportunity presents itself. Some people who have the right opportunities and circumstances are a little better than others who thus manifest the knowledge and energy, the Brahma force, and the human mental force.

Indian yogis say that there are 72000 Nadis in the human body. These nadis are very subtle and spread throughout your body. All these are related to Brahma force. These 72,000 nadis help each individual to tune into their mental thoughts.

What is Nadi?

A nadi is a pulse that runs through a nerve. Nadi has no physical existence. Nadi is a kind of energy that spreads prana in the body.

When mental force is generated by thought and manifests in less than a second, the electromagnetic force participates in all the atoms, nadi, and nerves in the body (electromagnetic force). The energy emanating from them energizes the basic effects of thought, cause, matter, and time. It is manifested in the brain as alpha, beta, gamma, delta, and beta waves according to your thoughts. Energy attuned to these waves manifests as human power. Frequencies evolve to match your thoughts.

Your brain contains nerve cells. They fire electrical signals day and night. This creates a unique arrangement called a brain wave pattern. These very unique patterns are intimately connected to your thoughts, emotions, moods, biochemistry, everything you do, and literally everything you are. - Eco institute.org

How life energy, other forces, many colors, etc. are hidden in the sunlight and activities emerge. Likewise, mental energy is latent in the mind and emerges during action energy.

Just as we have a mind, the cosmic mind is one. Somehow in the individual, there is the same in the universe. The universe has a physical body. After that is the Suksuma body. Then the universe has a mind. Then there is the universal I-consciousness. Then there is universal knowledge. All these are natural. Everything is an expression of nature and is not outside of it. It has an infinite reservoir of mind energy that is limitless. It is from this that we are relentlessly drawing mental energy. This is because all our minds are part of the Universal Mind. From this universal mind, man gets what he deserves according to his actions. The Universal Mind provides the right mental force in the right way, to the right man. The Universal Mind does not hesitate to provide this for human use according to its purpose. It has its pros and cons. The universal mind gives this to individuals according to their mental nature.

It is usually formed into thought and transformed into energy by the nature of human reasoning. From the characteristic of each thought arises the corresponding energies. Undoubtedly the most highly developed personal skill of man at his present stage of evolution is the rational systematization of inner and outer life by means of cognitive determination. It is the King because it is the individual higher skill of ruling itself over the complexities of our human existence. It is this reasoning that distinguishes man from other terrestrial creatures and accounts for his evolution and biological renaissance.

The power of an individual's mind force depends on his personal characteristics. Our body has a role in this. It also depends on the body and knowledge received from our parents. It depends on the individual. As much as the individual feels to use mind force, so much power is gained. The Universal Mind is waiting to bestow upon an individual human being unlimited undivided powers depending on his intentions. Individuals who have been able to do this for many years have cultivated themselves and their dependent people by using it. Our world history has recorded people who received these extraordinary powers in front of our eyes. As far as India is concerned, there are many people who have learned the very rare psychic arts of cosmic power. The mind cannot act on its own. It is only with the help of the soul that the mind can bring about its movement in this universe.

The challenge of explaining consciousness (mind) as a physical process is, I suggest, by recognizing that the brain operates based on the principle of dynamic processing. Neurons, along with other material systems such as astrocytes and mitochondria, have highly organized pathways to drive behaviors critical to the survival of the organism. This makes sense when we consider the fact that living things live in a physical world structured on energy, forces, and work that transform, distribute, and dissipate (diffusion, electrostatics). To survive and thrive in this world, they must constantly work to obtain new supplies of high-quality or free energy to maintain an internal state far from thermodynamic equilibrium. (Boltzmann, 1886; Schrödinger, 1944; Schneider and Sagan, 2005). In addition to internal regulation, nervous systems help organisms perform two main tasks: sensing environmental conditions such as temperature, acidity, salinity, nutrient levels, or the presence of predators. Discrimination between variations and shifts toward environmental conditions is beneficial for survival. Harmful). -

If consciousness is a natural physical process, it must be explained in terms of energy, forces, and work. Energy is a physical property of nature. It is functional and, like forces and work, may be regarded as real differences of motion and tension.

Evidence from neurobiology indicates that the brain operates on the principle of energetic processing and that a specific energetic structure in the brain can reliably predict the presence and extent of consciousness using information theoretic techniques. Since energy is efficient in physical systems, it is reasonable to say that consciousness is in principle caused by energetic activity and how it is dynamically organized in the brain.

Information in a biological environment is best understood as a measure of the way dynamic activity is organized, i.e. its complexity or degree of differentiation and integration. Information theoretic techniques provide powerful tools for measuring, modeling, and mapping a system of dynamic processes, but we should not confuse mapping with territory.

Real differences, as distinguished from the abstract differences represented in mathematics and information theory, are characterized by the fact that there is something to undergo those differences, that is, to undergo opposing states of opposite forces. All true difference is like this, so not all contribute to consciousness. It has been proposed that a specific type of activity occurs in the human brain that causes our conscious experience. It is a specific dynamic system of dynamic processes with a high degree of differentiation and integration. This system recursively results in a form of self-referential and energetic activity those blossoms into a level of complexity sufficient for consciousness.

If consciousness (mind) is a physical process, and physical processes are driven by real differences of motion and tension, then there is something like undergoing real differences organized in a particular way in the brain, which is what we intrinsically experience -

Thanks

(Frontiersin.org/articles/10.3389/spyg.2018.02091/full)

All energies in the universe have been generalized by Indian yogis as prana (dark energy in modern times). The sky is mind.The sky itself manifests as matter. The activity of Prana Shakti or Prana Energy pervades the entire universe. When the activity of this prana is very subtle, the sky becomes mind. Even there it is an indivisible block. Even if you reach that subtle level, you can see and feel that this universe is made up of subtle vibrations. Today's modern nuclear scientists are using string theory to look inside atoms and prove that they are ultimately in a state of micro-vibration. So the mind gets the key through the subtle vibration of prana (dark energy). Through prana, the mind energy works together with the brain.

The universe has a very high connection with human beings. If aliens exist we cannot know their knowledge of the universe. Matter (Matters) All other created beings have motions, evolution, and dimensional evolutions according to a finite law, and therefore never, in the least, change from such actions. Aliens may know a mind unknown to us and keep it in motion in many ways. Living beings, material objects, appear, exist, and perish. Its cosmic activities stop with these. All creations other than man are bounded by the 4 fundamental forces. Only man is capable of perceiving the first mental force or mind force which is fundamental. Man can use all five types of forces. Mental force (mana energy) manifests as an energy.

The sages who reveal deep spiritual truths to mankind gain their wisdom through direct association with those true vibrations. All other inventions that man has made and will make in the future are vibrating in their embryonic space. When an inventor works the mental force correctly he is attuned to intuitively receive the conceptual vibration for the creation of his invention. That is, he is motivated to acquire it by mental force or mental energy. An inventor can be said to have found a new invention. But nothing really new was discovered. This he has only done to reveal what was already hidden in the vibration state of the Barendum. A true case of the above-explained can be illustrated by an example.

Adolescent Genius by John Jay O'Neill is explained. In it, as a scientist, Niccolo discovered the theory of alternating current (AC). His and current devices are responsible for the inventions that are important factors in AC and today's electrical equipment and mechanical industrial systems. In 1882, Nikola Tesla was walking in a Budapest city park at dusk, reciting a poem, when suddenly Tesla

Frozen in a state of shocked ecstasy, his friend was terrified. At that moment, Tesla began to talk about an inner vision.

Watch me and watch me turn it, he repeated in an excited voice. His friend thought he was unwell. Tesla said he was actually looking at the alternator in action. I have found a solution to the problem. Can't you see it running almost silently right here in front of me now? People will no longer be slaves to hard work and my motor will set them free. He said it would do the work of the world. Over the next few months Blueprint continued to elaborate on the detailed preliminary forms he had in mind. Six years were imprinted on his mind until he put them into practical use. Thus no one can deny that Tesla's mind force combined with cosmic mind force produced a great invention.

We also know that the greatest power lies in the fineness itself and not in the matters. Fine nerves carry energy from something finer than themselves. It derives its energy from the thought of something far more subtle than itself. In reality, there is all energy in the subtlety(tiny).- Swami Vivekananda.

The greatest yogis have ended their lives on earth by uniting their mental force with the cosmic force. Without undergoing any chemical change, the same body is kept in the same state as it came from when it leaves the living body. It is in tune with their cosmic mind force and they reach this state. Paramahamsa Yogananda attained Maha Samadhi on March 7, 1952, in Los Angeles, USA. From March 7th to March 27th, when he left the body, everyone saw that no chemical disturbance or biological change took place in his body. It was a great surprise and a rare event for everyone.

There is a great reason for this: Paramahamsa Yogananda united himself with the cosmic will and proved it by praying that the people of the world should feel its energy and pride in this event by using the cosmic connection of his mental force to remain in a bond without undergoing physical chemical change after death. It is an essential thing.

Sri Aurobindo calls this power "Overmind".

He speaks of an even higher power, the "supermind."

He also wanted to bring,

And brought down, on earth.

These forces are difficult for us to understand.

But Sri Aurobindo's interpretation may help us a little.

He says "Supermind means

Absolute Truth - Divine Consciousness

Between the Supermind and the human mind

a number of ranges, planes….

The Overmind is the highest of these limits;

It is full of light and powers…"

He said, "The Overmind must be reached and overthrown

Before Supermind discipline is possible-

Because Overmind is the passage…"

No doubt we cannot grasp these things.

The ordinary mind is very limited.

This higher power, Sri Aurobindo says of this in Savitri.

A man's mind force interacts with these and brings energy.

1. Brahma mind force and prana.

1. Brahma Force Correlation
2. Human mind force communication
3. Prana communication
4. Parabrahmam communication
5. Super Mind communication
6. Spatial communication
7. Natha level (vibration) communication
8. Atma Siddhi status communication

2. Man's mind force

Manas, Ahankara, Buddhi, Chitta

1. Conscious
2. Subconscious mind

3. The highest level of consciousness or supermind.

4. Physical energy

5. Psychological power

6. Thought

7. Deep thinking

8. Actions

9. Powerful thought

10. Self-learning brings power

11. Mantra

12. Tantra

13. Yantra

14. Word

15. Writing

16. Form, creative work

17. Meditation:

1. Awareness

2. Transcendence

3. Spiritually exciting experiences

4. Paramananda

5. Breath

6. Intuitive stage controlling external perception

   Eithal or reaching (Controlling the external senses and reaching the intuitive level)

7. Changes occur in the human mind, body, brain,and nervous systems

8. Achieving a state of deep peace and silence

9. Enlightenment

18. Prayer

19. Ashta Siddhis

20. Memories

21. Curiosity about cosmic Nature

22. Brain and associated organs.

23. Electromagnetic force.

24. Gravity force
25. Strong nuclear force
26. Weak nuclear force
27. Photon
28. Mind vibration
29. Vibration or sound
30. Electromagnetic waves
31. Brain waves
32. Molecules
33. Chemical substances
34. Foods
35. Metaphysics (Mind And Matter)
36. Quantum physics
37. Theory of Vibration
38. Cosmic Energy
39. Vital movement
40. Presumptive power
41. Superconsciousness

The psychic power to cure the disease:

1. Pray to Jesus for healing

2. Reiki and prayer

3. Yogananda's healing prayer

Techniques. What are the powers of the other senses?

1. Extrasensory perception ESP:

ESP is a sense beyond the senses. (Extrasensory Perception) It is a psychic power that is perceived by the mind as thoughts, information, past events, future events, and present events that are not received through the senses by an individual human instinct or by the instinct of a powerful person.

In India, it is a subject that has been introduced since ancient times. We call it enlightenment. Maharishis, Yogis, Mahans, Siddhars, and Jnanis, who have pure souls in India, have received the power of this Jnana Drishti. Not only in ancient times but even in the twentieth century, many sages have used this power of wisdom in India. This is what is now called extra-sensory perception in modern times. Some prophets, not only in India but also in other countries, foretell events beyond the senses to such.

Also, we will know about it in the section titled Meditation Power of Yogis. So here too we can realize that the mind force energy that is the subject of our book plays a part here.

2. **Intuition:** Intuition is the pre-notification of an event through your subconscious mind.

You may face some hardships when you defy this intuitive declaration. This intuition is often about you, about an event, about the troubles of your relationships, and about the actions of your individual soul, predicting future events before they happen to you. Intuition tells you the pros and cons of an action and its consequences when you initiate it, but is your choice. i.e. your mind. Sometimes it can be beneficial if you go against that intuition's prompting.

Intuition is the discriminating faculty that allows you to decide which of two reasonings is right. Right intuition makes you the master of all knowledge. A strong-willed person usually has active intuitive power. You have to develop latent intuitive teachers; this can only be realized more through meditation).- Yogananda .com

3. Telepathy: For those who believe that telepathy is the expression of thoughts by the mind without speech, the first scientific institution has received through modern science that there are invisible rays that actually go from one person to another.

All this energy is generated from Brahma mind force through human mental force connection.

4. Mind vibration:

1. Mind force, brain, and particles always be connected with Brahma mind force.

2. The force of the mind is contact with a nearby person or a person who is far away.

3. Strings of all cosmic activity. Your brain, mind, and body all vibrate with certain thoughts. Always it is a vibrational record, no one can erase it.

4. Through the mental force energy of wisdom one can easily perceive an action through wavelength communication and frequencies. The energy of the Brahma Mind to reach past, present, and future waves and wavelengths of mental energy through enlightenment is given the potential.

5. The waves of the particular thought should be capable of taking a coherency in those with whom the thought communicates at the same level.

6. The ordinary man is given the opportunity to complete or achieve the karmic action of these three force vibrations of the mind, past, present, and future.

7. Anger's wavelength will easily connect with people who are close to the same wavelength. The same goes for other activities. Example: lust, love, happiness

8. Temple, Church, Mosque, all these can easily bring pure vibrational thoughts to your mind.

9. With the power of your pure mind, you can draw from it intelligence, energies, wisdom, goodness, subtle individuality, individual humanity, and intuition as the cosmic vibrations align.

10. Man seeks to understand the secret of the mind and the natural laws of matter by dissecting and perceiving their detectable molecules, essential constituents, dominant forces, etc. But these are not easily distinguishable. However, the cosmic mind enables man to understand the secrets of his historical evolution, whose intrinsic meaning and value are shrouded in a thick veil by the systematic investigation or effort of his individual mind force.

Chapter 32

What is self-realization?

Self-realization is the realization that a human being is one in body, mind, and soul with God's omnipresence. It is the influence of mind force that a superior human being can feel. To get a feeling for this, man can improve his emotional knowledge of the universe.

You are that:

Everything that exists in the universe came into existence through the power of the Paramatma, It is the form of consciousness or Brahma force that is the cause of all things. Hydrogen is formed from it and water is formed from it. Creatures and man are made of water. Man is made of water. A man came alive to live on earth through the contact of the first primordial hydrogen atom. Also, humans and other organisms have many types of molecules present in their bodies. Man breathes oxygen to live. Carbon dioxide (CO2) for plants to live and light from the sun are all from the universe. It's in you. The relation of Brahma force is to man. The power of the Brahman mind and the power of the human mind are united. It has been proven. Therefore, the universe is you.

Source: Our body consists of 60 percent to 70 percent water. 75 percent of our brain is made up of water. Water is the lifeblood of life on earth. The scriptures very clearly confirm that You are that. Water (H2O) was created from the first primordial atom, hydrogen.

The universe expanded and cooled from the superheated flaming state, or the instant of origin, when the Big Bang occurred. As the universe cooled many changes took place in space.

In particular, elementary particles, quarks, and electrons were created. Then protons and neutrons were created. As the temperature of the flame decreased over another 380,000 to 500,000 years, the electrons became attached to the atoms. This created hydrogen and helium atoms. These are light gases. Hydrogen gas is flammable and explosive. Helium is an inert gas. The first atom of hydrogen evolved into a second atom of helium. This is a very important event. Hydrogen and helium combine to form clouds that over time form galaxies, stars, and other matter resulting from stellar nucleosynthesis, elements, and life. At vast expansion, 73% hydrogen and 25% helium. Its isotopes are responsible for many cosmic matters, including the Sun and Earth. Helium atoms are present on Earth's surface.

Hydrogen and helium make up 70% and 28% of the Sun, respectively. Hydrogen gas is the primary cause of water formation on Earth. That is, one oxygen atom in a water molecule is bonded to two hydrogen atoms. This causes water. Water plays an important role in the origin of life on Earth. Hydrogen is a factor in the genetic makeup of DNA and RNA in the human body. Three of the stars (triple) - due to the alpha process, carbon nuclei combine with additional helium to form stable isotopes of oxygen and energy. It should be mentioned here that the source of all is hydrogen.

Helium, for some reason, contributes to the formation of oxygen. Thus atoms like hydrogen and helium are important factors in the origin of the universe. Discovery of Hydrogen and Helium:

The lightest element hydrogen (gas) was discovered in 1766 by physicist Henry Cavendish. Helium gas was discovered in 1868 by the French astronomer Jules Johnson. While conducting astronomical research in India, he observed a yellow line in the solar eclipse spectrum. This was the first evidence of helium. Chemist Edward Frankland named the element responsible for this yellow line Helios. Later it was called helium gas.

Therefore, according to the scriptures, it is fully true that you are that. The power of the Brahma mind and the power of the human mind are the same.

We know how energy resides in the microcosm of the universe. All material objects and living beings are created from something microscopic. Similarly, here Hearing, Touch, Sight, Taste, and Smell are subtle than the senses. The mind is finer than the Tanmatras; the intellect is more subtle than the mind. Avyaktam (Mula Prakrti) is more subtle than Atma. More subtle than this is Purusha or Brahman.

The universe revealed itself to the supreme yogis who had turned inward. Thus one with universal knowledge. As a result, they did many things that an ordinary person would not be able to do. The ability to penetrate the minds of others, use supernatural powers, help other people by using their powers, transmit their powers to others as light, cure diseases, eliminate other grievances consider the good of others as important, concentrate the mind, and use subconscious and also, They are capable of performing events such as concealing themselves using, revealing themselves, and revealing their identity to the right people i.e. to those who are capable of bearing their vagaries.

This is how normal human beings have used their subconscious energy to do countless things. The knowledge of all the variations in the world is caused by this instinct. When everyone works with their mental energy in a unified state of trust, you get what you strive for. If you study human history, everything happened because of the perfect use of the ray of mental force. We know that people who are weak in sub consciousness don't do anything right. But the mind energy of yogis and the mental energy of people like us is different in its nature. It is the duty of every human being born on this earth to attain his higher psychic power, self-realization, and know the truth about him.

Chapter 33

Energy:

Energy is reality, and the First Great Law expresses the essence of the governing nature of the universe.

Energy is the fundamental measure of the universe's ability to perform physical activity. It can be in different forms (mechanical, thermal, etc.) and it can transform from one form to another. It cannot come out of nowhere, it cannot disappear here now.- National Research Nuclear University MEPhi (National Research Nuclear University) MEPhi (Moscow Engineering Physics Institute)

All energy in this universe is hidden in space. It manifests itself when the appropriate medium approaches or contacts it and when it is at a distance. Energy is also converted into different forms of motion when it is thus released i.e. converted into kinetic energy. This energy multiplies itself. Thus it has continuous energy. Specifically, kinetic energy manifests itself in a variety of ways in a cycle that changes from thermal motions to cold state motions and back again. It participates in this movement of energy as life and material. Energy in general manifests an action potential when it comes into motion in this cosmic action. That is energy. All motion is energy. This can be interpreted as kinetic energy.

The force of mind manifests as energy in living beings. In humans, this manifests as a subtle energy different from the energy of the material.

To explain consciousness (mind) as a physical process, we must acknowledge the role of energy in the brain. Energetic activity is fundamental to all bodily processes and drives biological behavior. Recent neurological evidence can be interpreted to indicate that consciousness (mind) is a product of dynamic activity in the brain. However, the nature of energy remains largely mysterious, and we do not fully understand how it contributes to brain function or consciousness. According to the theory outlined here, energy, along with forces and work, can be described as actual differences in motion and tension. By observing physical systems, we can infer something like undergoing real differentiation from an intrinsic perspective of the system.

Neurons in the brain respond to actions by repeating messages along its pathways and forming new connections:

Neurons in the brain repeatedly send messages along their pathways and form new connections as you continue to perform your learning activities and begin to perform a new activity. Due to this, there is a change in your mind force state and a change in energy comes into action. Likewise, your brain changes its structure when every new thought you learn, action, and memory occurs. That means making connections of new neurons. Thus the thoughts of your mind, the activities of the brain, and the resulting causal actions take their final form as energy through mental impulses. Similarly, meditation, calm atmosphere, stress relief, mental unity, focus, new thinking, motivation, individuality, perseverance, eagerness to learn new things, exercise, happiness, and some other qualities help to bring energy to your mind or you.

According to the activities in the brain, the millivoltage voltage (-mv) is different for the cell membrane i.e. rest and activity. On both sides of the cell membrane are molecules of proteins, sugars, and the entire host of charged ions. These can be positive and negative. The energy of the brain is based on this.

Swami Vivekananda explains the scientific concept of this energy very clearly through his wisdom in Heroic Languages Part Three:

Here one can know cosmic energy and introverted traits.

This universe is the body of the Lord, this body shrinks from the nature of thula or matters and becomes subtle and becomes the root cause of the universe. While others say this about the Universe, that the Advaitis say that the Lord becomes this universe. A subtle question arises here. We and all the things we see are God! becomes Yes. This book is Lord, everything is Lord; my body is Lord, my mind is Lord, my soul is Lord. Then why should there be so many lives? Has the Lord divided into these millions? Has that one God become so many millions of lives? Otherwise, how could there be so many lives? How could God, who is the only substance of the universe, who is perfect energy and matter, become so divided? The infinite cannot be separated. How does the pure Lord become, the universe? If he himself became the universe, he is changeable in nature. A changer is a part of nature. A thing of natural and changing nature has both birth and death. If our Lord is also of a changeable nature, he must be destroyed by you. Consider this well. Well, how many parts of God has become this universe? If it is assumed that it is a (An unknown quantity) part, now God has decreased to the amount of a; that is God-a (God minus a) now, so God after creation is not God before creation. Because a part of him has become the universe. So Advaitis, the universe is not what we see, it is just an illusion. This universe is gods, angels, and other living beings that are born and die in this world come and go. Souls say that everything is a dream. There is no life. How can there be so many beings? There is only one infinite. The same sun appears multiple when reflected in multiple bodies of water. Millions of drops of water show the same sun as millions of suns. Every visible image is a flawless image of the sun. Even though millions of images appear like this, in reality, there is only one sun. In this way, all living beings reflect the same Lord in many minds. Minds, like drops of water, reflect this One Absolute. Lord is reflected in these many living beings. Although a dream, a reality must come into existence through it. That true substance is the Lord who is the substance of infinite perfection. The artificial you of body, mind, and life is just a dream.

But your true form is Truth-Knowledge-Enjoyment. You are the lord of this universe. You yourself create this entire universe and again subdue it within yourself. This is what Advaita says. So births, rebirths, comings, and goings are all illusions. You are infinite, you can go anywhere. The sun, the moon, and all this universe are mere drops of your nature that subdue everything. How can you be born or die? I was never born; I will not be born. I had no mother, no father, no friends, no enemies. Because I am the object of perfect truth knowledge. I am him, I am him.

Vedanta philosophy is three steps up. We cannot go further than this. How can this science go beyond the oneness of all being one, but once it has reached the oneness, it cannot go beyond it for any reason? We cannot go beyond this concept of perfection. Not everyone can follow this Advaita philosophy. It's tough. At first, it is difficult to understand with common sense. It requires very sharp knowledge, courage, and clarity. In order to know a little of the universe, the contact of the Brahma mind force is necessary, how to get this energy? We can learn about the finer things of creation through science. Man can acquire cosmic knowledge and make new inventions with the power of his mind. This also requires cosmic energies like light, sound, electromagnetism, electrical equipment, human mind power, and many scientific principles.

Also, the knowledge that is enhanced in cosmic knowledge can be achieved through the awareness of human intuition. In India, this is called enlightenment, inner awareness, or the state of spiritual consciousness. Those who attain the state of spiritual consciousness acquire great powers.

Through thought to the human mind, it emerges as instinct and becomes a mind force. Many are the forces that have been at work to shape the destiny of this human race and are still at work. Among these forces, the religious forces are the most effective in the human mind. Here man directed his quests into the inner world. Then man became engrossed in the research of various states of mind. He discovered that he was in a higher state than the dream and memory states.

All major religions refer to these states as ecstasy or inspiration, a state of inner awareness. Through this man gets the energies from God and uses them for the betterment of mankind.

Most have learned that even though they struggle to attain this power, they cannot attain it through the senses. Infinite bliss cannot be attained through the senses. That is, they know that the finite senses and body cannot express the infinite. Whenever a man becomes one with a pure settled soul, nature realizes that pure soul and reveals its nature to him. Another systematic instinct is that man develops that power through science. Here it is achieved with the help of cosmic Brahma mental force.

It has a corresponding effect according to the mind force expressed by human instinct. Man thus introduces a new invention to the world. According to the material discovered, its energy develops, expands, multiplies, and benefits. It has been working since the beginning without energy and forever.

We can clearly see how the thoughts of the human mind act as impulses through the brain and end up with energy through the following action. example;

If I want to reach for a tumbler full of water on a table, I first look at the tumbler full of water and its information. Here, first through my eyes, that is, through the retina, through the optic nerve, this information will go inward, through a relay station called the thalamus in the middle of the brain, then the occipital cortex at the back of the brain will communicate with the information processing, and then the information will be at the forefront of decision-making, and finally movement It sends signals to the hubs. They travel down the spinal cord to the tip of the body and then communicate with the tumbler full of water, where the sensation is focused again on the tumbler full of water, and then it goes to the spinal cord and back to the brain and, also to the sensory centers of the brain. Here you will feel the magnificence of the great work of this brain. There you reach out and grab the tumbler.

If we focus our attention here, we can realize or know with amazement how the most wonderful activity of the brain, precisely and rapidly, is done through electrical signals (activity) in motion.

That is, the entire nervous system of the human body is involved in it. It is considered one of the remarkable features of the brain. There are basically two actions here. As a reference, whatever man sees on one side is reflected on the other side.

There are two reasons for this.

One, one side of the brain controls the opposite or opposite side of the body. Many of our senses and actions are coordinated in the same way. Thus a visual field is precisely bounded by one side of the visual field, and the opposite by the other side. One of its properties is that you can do reasonable damage. There are still no major flaws with this brain. People can get along very well with the loss of large parts of the brain. One side of our body or a small part of our body may have defects.

Nature's evolution has made it an excellent system that is very strong and resilient. As humans, we know that we are distinctly different in this. Most of what differentiates humans here is in their hands. I think that's enough for now. We know that a particular action works in the human body and brain.- David Cox reflects their opinion.

Gurudeva can attach himself to the mind of any human being with whatever he desires. His powers and thoughts act as a human radio. (A yogic power mentioned in Patanjali Yoga Sutras 111:19)

Some mottos of Swami Vivekananda about the power of mind;

1. Let people say whatever they want. Hold fast to your own firm resolve and then the rest will surely follow and the world will bow at your feet.

2. Man is bound by nothing but the rules he makes for himself.

3. The highest among men is he who can say that he knows everything about himself.

4. Strength is life and weakness is death.

5. If you don't believe in yourself, even if God comes in person, it's useless.

6. Only if our life is good and pure then the world can be good and pure.

7. Don't look back always look forward to what you want to do and you will surely progress.

8. All the powers you believe in yourself are within you. Realize it and you manifest that power and say I am capable of achieving anything.

9. Cowards and fools, this is my fate, but the mighty man dares to conquer that fate.

10. No power in the universe can stop someone from achieving what he is capable of achieving. Try till you finish.

11. You become what you think. If you think you are strong, you will be strong. Never think that there is anything that you cannot achieve.

12. Get up and stay awake and don't stop until you reach your goal.

13. Don't be afraid of burdens, the earth that carries this world is under your feet.

14. Don't worry about failures. Even if you slip away from the goal a thousand times, even if you make mistakes in working towards the goal, keep holding on to that goal again and again. Try 1000 times to achieve your goal even if you fail 1000 times try one more time Don't give up.

15. Man becomes wise through failure.

What does it bring spiritual energy to the mind?

Yoga, meditation, japa, prayer, etc. Learn about these in the next section.

Existence is energy. Science has discovered that what is observed is energy, material energy. Throughout the ages, for at least five thousand years, the other polarity has been known or perceived as the object, the observer, and the sentient energy.
Your body is energetic. Your mind is made up of energy.

The mind is a little more subtle, but not yet subtle because you can close your eyes and see thoughts moving. They can see. They don't look like your body. Your body is visible to all outsiders and is public. The action of your thoughts is personally visible. No one else can see your thoughts; You can only see them or those who have worked very deeply in seeing thoughts. But normally they are not visible to others. Yogis can read your mind. It takes a lot of hard work to get it. It blossoms or occurs when the soul's mind becomes pure.

The third, final layer within you is consciousness. It is not visible to you. It cannot be reduced to an object, it remains an object.

When these three forces work in harmony, you will be healthy and whole. If these energies are not working harmoniously, the force of the mind will work in conflict, with the mind. body, the emotions will not be coordinated and controlled, and the body will become sick and unhealthy. You are no longer complete. Also, perfection must be sacred.

When your body, mind, and consciousness are all in one rhythm, unifying, in deep harmony, not conflicting, but succeeding in your effort to cooperate, the moment your body, mind, and consciousness work together, you have become a trinity, and the experience is divine. Osho. Thank you.

For example Swami Vivekananda, Paramahamsa Yogananda, and Dickinson (Mr. DICKINSON). Correspondence evidence of yogis. The power of the mind can be proved through empirical evidence of yogis. Forty-three later that event was confirmed.

We will know about this miracle in the next part of this book.

Chapter 34

When does man forget his mind?

Tavam is the state in which the mind hides itself in the place from which the power of 'I' arises. Tavam is the mind hiding itself in the sound of some mantra - Ramana Maharishi.

If asked to say only in Samadhi Yamadi

Eight siddhis are in Samadhi Yamadi

On that day for those who stayed in Samadhi Yamadi

Samadhi is itself exposed.

Samadhi is the state of yoga where one forgets the body and sinks into God without consciousness or memory. In meditation, the senses are suppressed and the desires are forgotten. In order to get the benefits of meditation and meditation, one should go beyond the limits of meditation engage in

Tavayoga, and pass the eight stages. For those who are engaged in meditation and penance, attaining the state of samadhi is attainable or possible to benefit from both - Yogi Thirumoolar.

Yogis unite the force of mind with the force of Brahma and Prana to reach the sublime state of consciousness called samadhi. In this way, man forgets his mind. The resulting forgetfulness is different from brain damage.

Chapter 35

Soul:

Every human being is made up of three parts – the body, the anthakarana or mind, and behind that the soul. The external covering of this soul is the body, the innermost mind, and in fact, the soul perceives and experiences everything. It is the soul, which drives the body through the mind.

In the human body, the non-material is the soul. Since it is not material, intellectually it cannot be composite. Therefore, being non-composite, it is not subject to causal laws. So it is imperishable, something imperishable cannot have a beginning. The soul is also formless. Everything that is material has form. Anything that does not depend on material matter cannot have form. Anything that has form must have a definite beginning and end. No one can have seen anything that has no beginning and no end. Energy and material form together. A certain amount of force acts on the material to shape it. Material power is formed by the combination of these two. This combination cannot be permanent. The time that separates each matter will come to an end. So all metaphors have a beginning and an end. Since the soul is formless, it does not follow the rules of origin and end, it has existed from infinite time. Just as time is eternal, so is the soul.

According to Advaita Vedanta, the soul within everyone is omnipresent, in you and in me. As we are on Earth, so we are still in the sun. You are in America. You are also in England. But it is through the body and the mind that the soul works, and wherever the body and mind are present, the work of the soul is evident.

Since the mind (force) is made of a very subtle material, it does not perish so quickly. Because the subtler an object is made of, the more stable it is. In the course of time, the mind also perishes. Those forces called Prana form the body and the mind out of material matter. Later on, when this mind also perishes and scatters into dust and leaves no samskaras behind, we attain perfect freedom.

The soul has no ebb and flow. It has no birth or death. Nature is the former of the soul and its functioning. The entire universe existed in Brahman.Emerged from it. It is operating only to be absorbed into that from which it emerged. It is like the electric power emitted from a dynamo completing a circuit and being reabsorbed into the dynamo. Such is the case with the soul. Various types emerge from it.Born as plants and animals, and finally born as a human being. Human birth is the closest birth to Brahman. Swami Vivekananda

The word mind in a broad sense is a state of consciousness within the human being i.e. the soul. Its intellect is used to mean inherent powers, willpower, and consciousness. By contrast, the term mind refers to the object defined as a consciousness like a mirror that receives and reflects impressions from the senses. They are then interpreted by knowledge, counteracted by feeling, and responded to by will(eetcha force).- Paramahamsa Yogananda.

Chapter 37

What are the differences between soul perception and body perception?

The sense of soul:

- Introspection is characteristic

Peaceful. it's an instinct. Action realized resistance. Feeling of Note. Purity. Freedom.

Non-violence is emotional. The soul is stays away and can observe the actions in the consciousness. It is stable. Cannot see by eye. Powerful. Atman is eternal. The Soul is immortal.

Space and time are not control. Beginning and Endless.

The sense of being:

- Outward-looking.
- Peaceless.
- Common feeling.
- Counteraction understanding.
- Sensing Command.
- External sense affected by others.
- Becomes attached to everything.
- Feeling disturbed.

- The body gets caught up in consciousness is unstable.
- Objectivity is powerful.
- The body is perishable.
- The body is temporary.
- The eye can see the body.
- Bound by space and time.
- Has origin and end.
-

Brahma mental force and human mental force are related to both soul consciousness and body consciousness.

Chapter 37

Mind, Brain, Soul:

The brain is the vehicle for the mind, and the horse is the living body. The path of this carriage is the emotions of life. Its destination is energy, movement, and creativity. It is the soul that drives the chariot.

The mind is composed of three layers. The first in this layer is made up of thoughts. This is the first superficial layer. Next to this is the second layer of emotions. This layer is slightly deeper than the previous one. But not deep enough. The third layer is the most important. This layer represents the act of silence. A state without sounds, without thoughts, and without feelings. The first layer is related to the head, i.e. the brain. The second layer depends on the heart. The third layer is also the state where we ourselves are subconscious.- Osho

1. To the mind, the brain nerves carry the record. After this, the mind creates the reaction.

2. If the mind does not understand the opposite action, we do not know the emotion. It is through this action that enlightenment occurs.

3. Mind is not the only cause. There is a force behind the mind. When the mind is set in motion like any other fundamental force it manifests as energy

4. The mind is the instrument of thought. Behind the mind is the soul. The mind is the instrument of the soul. The mind is the instrument of the soul. It

acquires experiences by interacting with the external organs of the eye, ear, nose, mouth, and body. These traps carry sensations to the senses. It is the inner senses, the centers of the brain, that are responsible for real experience.

5. Part of the cosmic power is the human soul. Thus the cosmic energy, soul, mind, brain, body, and external objects are interconnected.

6. Soul and mind are immortal.

7. The power of the human mind is that it observes and discerns, and like the marvelous world is ever-changing.

8. Our mental energy thoughts created this universe and therefore it is the Lord.

9. The word 'I' belongs to the soul. Atma is devoid of all evils such as casteism. Hence it is said that one.

10. The senses are subtle because the mind is not known by them. Atma Gnana itself is form and pure. Gnanendriyas are made up of the Mind and Intellect and Suksuma body.

11. If there is no soul, the mental force will not work in humans, animals, reptiles, birds, or aquatic creatures.

12. The mind belongs to the soul. It depends on living things. But the mind is not the soul. The soul is different and the mind is different.

13. The mind is related to the magnetic field.

14. The mind has vibrations. Each individual has their own set of mind vibrations.

15. Mind force is associated with atoms.

16. The mind force or mental energy of life strives to become what it depends on. In its nature, it is conducted in it and goes on its path.

17. Mind creates creation and can see its creation. Einstein explains the electromagnetic wave energy of light. The energy of each particle of light is related to the frequency of the wave. Acts as both a particle and a wave.Second, the photon is now considered a particle, a wave, and an excitation-type field. A quantum field, like electromagnetism, is a form of energy and potential that propagates through space.

18. The mental force works based on the parts of the brain such as the forebrain, cerebral cortex, nucleus, midbrain, hindbrain, thalamus, hypothalamus, pons, spinal cord, spinal cord, and the entire nervous system of the body.

19. During mental energy, the electrical impulse of the human body spreads throughout the body and emerges

as energy for processing with the help of the brain. This takes place through the nerves of the brain and the nerves of thc respective nervous systems which have connections to the respective parts of the body.

20. Psychic force acts like quantum theory by absorbing and emitting energy.

21. Soul and Mind In connection, neurons in the brain are entangled with many subatomic particles in the universe. They also transmit electrical signals. Therefore, causality takes place.

22. The soul passes from the subtle to the subtle, and from that to the subtle, by its karmic merits, gradually, gradually, in each birth, and attains the nature-fixed goal of ultimate self-realization or bliss (Brahman). Mind and body are vehicles for this.

23. You cannot invent anything new to attain absolute salvation by the power of the mind.Because the scriptures have given the answer. Also, you can never go beyond a complete unity of knowledge and ambition. The answer is tat dvam asi which means you are that. Modern science has come close to this.

24. Yoga teaches that subtle spiritual centers in the brain are the seat of the soul's human life and divine consciousness. They are Sahasrara, the thousand-petalled lotus at the apex of the cerebrum, the seat of cosmic consciousness; Kudostha, center between the

eyebrows, Christ seated in consciousness; And the spinal cord (connected by magnetic attraction to the Kudostha) is the seat of the higher consciousness; life and consciousness descend from these higher spiritual centers of consciousness into the body and flow down the trunk through the five subtle spinal cord centers and outward into the physical organs of life, cognition, and action. Branches flow. To regain the rapturous wisdom of his union with God, man's soul must ascend the sacred trunk and reach its home, the higher centers of God-consciousness located in the brain. It means that the soul itself has to go back up through the path it came down from. This can be accomplished through systematic and intensive practice, such as learning the scientific techniques of Yoga method meditation as taught by the Guru.- Sri Sri Paramahamsa Yogananda (Man's Eternal Quest Part-1)

25. Mind is a subtle expression.But powerful. The mind can appear alive and physical. It is the electric or liquid life (chemical life) and the solid gross body (cell body) mind invisible man or soul. Life or Prana is the fluid mind. Also, the body is thick or bigger. It is a simple theory about the mind.

26. The mind is a reservoir of energy. When the mind acts, the force of the mind acts or accompanies it. Mind + Mind Force = Feelings + Actions + Human Energy + Cosmic Connection. Mind and mental energy cannot be separated. The most subtle energy called prana

cannot be separated. Likewise, mind and mental energy cannot be separated. Wherever there is a mind, there is mental energy.

Soul, elementary particle, string theory, quantum entanglement, ontology, philosophy, all general sciences, mental science, soul The force of the mind, the brain integrates with the force of the mind.

Chapter 39

Difference between mind and consciousness:

Mind

1. Materiality

2. The human mind of the soul exposes the energy.

3. Hard disk of the computer

4. Our mind is whole in body

5. Chemicals in the brain are sometimes not needed.

6. Mind is a vehicle.

7. Knowledge, thinking, memories, intuition, awareness, transcendence, and energy all are linked.

8. Mind is the pre-birth experience,

9. Depends on the inner world.

10. Mind depends on soul.

11. Mind does not need sense.

12. Mind with vibrations goes beyond the space.

13. The mind becomes a part of the activity

within the cosmic nature

14. The mind is free.

15. Mind is without atoms.

Feelings:

1. Biomaterials
2. Factor for actions.
3. The actions like a computer of consciousness

   Consciousness is separate.
4. Chemical in the brain for emotion Combinations are required.
5. It is the wheel of the vehicle.
6. All the consciousness's inner and outer actions.
7. Consciousness manifests these based on Karmic action as a medium.

8. Dependent on the external world.
9. Sensory and 36 thatuvams - dependent object.
10. Senses required.
11. Emotions with body vibrations, not the beyond.

- The individual soul will be its base.
- Controlled by the mind.
- Consciousness needs atoms.

Chapter 40

What are the three vibration levels of the human mind?

Activity: The activity is rapid vibration,

Idleness: Although Idleness has a dull vibrating,

Peaceful State: Peaceful has a very intense vibrating.

It is the soul that sits on a chariot. The body is the chariot. Horses are the sensations of the senses that come from the brain through the mind and through the senses. There the mind is like a bridle. Intellect is considered the driver here. When a man is a slave to his senses he is of this world. Here man's mental state is vibration, active (even with rapid vibration), sluggish (even with slow vibration), and he becomes a renunciation after suppressing his nature through his senses (with very intense vibration) (renunciation state).

For example:

If you hear a low frequency of 19 Hz you start to panic. You will feel relaxed and calm in the presence of 432Hz frequency. This 432Hz frequency has many healing effects on your mind and body. The human body responds to different frequencies. Our human body vibrates at a natural frequency of 7.5 Hz, which is very close to nature. Did you know that there is a certain frequency associated with a certain emotion? Emotion is Energy+Motion ie energy in motion.Frequency of different emotions. Higher frequency means higher vibration. Correspondence to higher energy level.Good emotions have high frequencies while bad emotions have low frequencies. In the enlightened state, the frequency is more than 700Hz, and the lower frequency of vibration is the same feeling only the lower energy is equal to 20 Hz. At frequencies like 700 Hz, our mind enters a state of super consciousness. Transcendental consciousness is the blissful state of self-bliss rather than running after worldly pleasures. realization. This egoic state is beyond the conscious and subconscious levels of the mind. Friends, I briefly found some interesting things that help us understand life in a better scientific way. Frequencies of peace and desire in particular caught my attention. The frequency of peace was observed to be the second highest frequency after enlightenment, indicating that peace is at a higher level than happiness and love. When you are peaceful, you vibrate at higher frequencies compared to someone who is in love or enjoying the pleasures of worldly things. So it is clear from science that attaining a state of peace is

We have already seen that vibrations, wavelengths, and frequencies are generated based on impulse to match the arising thoughts of your mind.

What is important to note here is that if a man is angry, his frequency will be 150 Hz. The same frequency applies to an opponent facing a state of anger. So the frequencies of two individuals or groups of people begin to vibrate at the same level. It manifests as action accordingly. The opponent also gets angry due to this. The frequencies of the emotions are related to the thoughts in you. His frequency is 600Hz when he is calm. Similarly, waves with higher frequency have shorter wavelengths and waves with lower frequency have longer wavelengths. Motor neurons in the human body begin to emit higher frequencies when an active information gathering is too short. According to this, it will be up to frequencies >200 Hz.

Chapter 41

The first creation in the universe:

The lotus flower was the first life created by the Brahma mind force that arose in the cosmic consciousness. The first life or visible creation in the universe was the lotus flower. We can confirm this from the comments of our ancestors. When Sri Vishnu was in the ocean due to the immense mind energy of the cosmic dancing God of India, from the divine nature of his consciousness, a large lotus flower appeared from the navel by the force of the Brahma mind of Sri Vishnu. Lord Brahma appeared in this lotus flower. The Lotus flower symbolizes wisdom. According to this, we know that the lotus flower was created in this universe before Lord Brahma. Therefore, the first life or visible creation in the universe was the lotus flower. Lord Brahma created the great universe and earthly creations.

Lord's mind, the great creation (Srushti), cosmic condensation, yoga, worship, mantra, cosmic philosophy, planets, gods, rishis, Siddhas, sages, sound, light, stories, kings, sages are described in historical genealogy. , and contains many theories. Goddesses in India have lotus flowers in their hands. Buddha is holding a lotus flower in his hand. Many civilizations have reported the virtues of the lotus flower. The Lotus flower is especially important in Indian culture, Egyptian culture, East Asian countries, etc.

In India, female deities are believed to be blessed by sitting on a lotus flower. I am referring to the lotus flower in the Sri Yantra engraved in the desert region of America by aliens. The shape of the lotus flower is prominent in Sri

Chakra. Sri Chakra explains Bhumi Tattva, one of the cosmic Tattvas.

A lotus stem is hidden in the lower part of the Bindu point at the center of the Sri Yantra. The stem is elongated and introverted. A lotus stalk is several billion light-years away. In one of its boundaries resides the cosmic creative power. Bindu is the center from which that boundless energy Sri Shiva Mahapurana and Sri Madbhagavata Mahapurana stand out among the oldest texts in India. Both these were blessed by Maharishi Vedavyasa. The Puranas have reached the present day through meditative and ancient leaf trails. Therefore, it is impossible to predict ancient ideas based on time. However, as an organized text, scholars date these to a common era of the 3rd to 12th century. These texts contain the lotus flower and glorious concepts related to it. In this book, the glorious energy of the primordial emerges. The universe comes into being when energy is released.

Chapter 42

Significance of Lotus Flower:

In the Bhagavad Gita, Krishna says that among flowers I am the lotus flower.

Lotus Specialty:

The lotus flower is revered and revered as sacred in Hinduism and Buddhism. The Lotus flower has the power to attract the beholders. It has a divine nature in itself.

Sublime Sundaram means beautiful. It has got beautiful colors. In this rose color (pink) lotus flower looks beautiful.Also available in red, white, yellow, purple, and purple colors. The national flower of India is the lotus flower.

In verse 844 of Yogi Thirumoolar in his book Thirumantram,

Action of matter, There is no water

A rootless lotus blossomed

There is a light that can be seen everywhere

No bottom, no top, in the question. That is the Lotus.

According to human knowledge, no grass or plant can grow without soil and water. Both terrestrial and aquatic plants have roots. Before the plant blooms, the first leaves and the flower blooms as a sequel. This lotus flower is blooming without soil and water. This lotus has no bud, no root, and no stem. However, this lotus flower has light. This flower has very Ancient (athi) no beginning, new no beginning, and no end. This Lotus has grown in Enlightenment.

The lotus is in water, i.e. it spreads out and spreads everywhere according to the surface of the water. Similarly, cosmic energy is spread throughout the universe depending on its output power in space. Lotus seeds have been able to germinate for up to 1300 years. It is the oldest flower, with fossils dating back 15 million years, scientists believe.

In fact, a University of California biologist found a seed with the ability to germinate in a dry lakebed in northeastern China. It is estimated to be almost 1300 years old.

Enlightenment occurs when a person attains the state of Duriyam or Sahasraharam with a thousand lotus petals on top of his head through meditation through mental force. The lotus flower is a symbol of meditation.

The Lotus flower is considered a great spiritual symbol. The lotus flower is the symbol of the Ramakrishna Mission, the Yogatha Satsang Society of India, and many other spiritual centers in India.

Such a glorious lotus flower, the lotus vine appeared in Sri Vishnu's navel by the power of the Brahma mind force before creation began. Lord Brahma appeared in it and started creation. This event is believed in by Hindu yogis and Hindu people of India.

Chapter 43

Do you know what the speed of your mind force is?

Brain cells called neurons send information and instructions to all parts of the brain and body. Information is transmitted by electrochemical signals called action potentials that travel down the length of the neuron. The neurons are then stimulated to release chemical ions called neurotransmitters. These act by stimulating the activity of nearby cells. These help the signal spread throughout the body. Although our thoughts and feelings, coldness, temperature, condition of the skin, muscle weakness, and tingling are the unaffected senses of man, and the affected senses, are divided into body size.So not all information is equally important and urgent. Especially the sensations that are felt through the skin on the body, rather than the pain in the internal parts of your body, transmit information immediately with the help of neurons. Some pain information sends signals at a speed of about 0.5-2.0m/s. According to the activity of some nerves, the information is faster. The reason is that neurons have two special characteristics. The information or signal is faster according to its diameter and the myelin sheath. The smaller the diameter. And information about the mail envelope is slow.

Now when a thought appears the sensory information received as action can be defined as the mental force and mental activity involved from that moment to the moment an action is initiated. Thinking in one's mind usually involves human interaction, activities of the five senses, various types of thoughts, and feelings, planning of actions, decision-making, and environmental, phenomena based on these processes. According to these ideas the speed of mental force depends on the interactions of complex networks of neurons throughout the peripheral and central nervous system.

Chapter 44

What is nerve conduction velocity?

Nerve conduction velocity (cv) is the speed at which an electrochemical impulse travels along a neural pathway. These conduction velocities are driven and influenced by a variety of factors including age, sex, and various medical conditions affecting body parts. Conduction velocities are specific to each individual and often fall within a limited range depending on the diameter of the axon and how well that axon is myelinated.

A few myelinated neurons in your brain normally travel at speeds of up to 120 m/s (m/s) (432 kilometers/hour or 275 miles (275 mph).

Corresponding parts of the nervous system are active according to many different thought processes. Based on the stimulation of those areas, nervous system information or electrical signals are rapidly transmitted throughout the body. All human thoughts are based on actions, the timing of which is ultimately shaped by the properties of neurons and their associated networks. The large-diameter myelinated neurons that connect the spinal cord to the muscles can travel at speeds of 156 to 270 miles per second (m/s) at 70 to 120 meters per second (m/s). The signals travel along the same path. And sensitive information is processed much faster. Recent research confirms that it takes only 20 to 30 milliseconds for an individual neuron to process a particular sensation. Normal impulses of the peripheral nerves of the legs are also 40 to 45 milliseconds. Similarly, sensory impulses in the peripheral nerves of the hands also travel at 50 to 65 milliseconds.

A typical time for neurons to respond to visual signals seen with one's hands is 0.28 seconds. For example, if a motor neuron presses a button after seeing a green light it takes about 0.28 seconds.

Research suggests that the normal conduction velocity for any given nerve is in the range of 50 to 60 milliseconds.

A. Motor fibers types of neurons:

Extrafusal muscle fibers have a conduction velocity of 50 to 60 milliseconds.

Intrafusal muscle fibers have a neuron conduction velocity of 4 to 24 milliseconds.

B. Sensory fiber types:

In Golgi tendons (proprioception), the conduction velocity of this type of neuron is 80 to 120 milliseconds.

Muscle spindle Secondary receptors Cutaneous mechanoreceptors All skin motor receptors have a conduction velocity of 33 to 75 milliseconds.

Touch and pressure nerve endings (free nerve endings) Nociceptors of the neospinothalamic tract (neospinothalamic tract) Cold thermoreceptors (cold thermoreceptors) Their neuron conduction speed is 3 to 30 milliseconds.

e. Autonomic effort fiber type:

Preganglionic fibers have a conduction velocity of 3 to 15 milliseconds, and postganglionic fibers have a conduction velocity of 0.5 to 2.0 milliseconds.

E. Peripheral nerves:

Median sensory means or their conduction velocity is 45 to 70 milliseconds

Median motor neurons have a conduction velocity of 49 to 64 milliseconds.

Tibial motor neurons have a conduction velocity of 41 plus milliseconds

Sural sensory neurons are 46 to 64 milliseconds.

There are also some peripheral nerves that have a nerve conduction velocity of 44 to 74 m/s.

Depending on the ability of your eyes to focus, you can see at a rate of one object per second with the power of the brain and mind. In that case, you can mentally locate 25 to 30 objects in an average of 30 seconds. Your mental force speed will be at this level. This means that you are mentally, physically, and mentally healthy.

In particular, the body's nerve conduction measurements vary based on an individual's age, gender, body temperature, limb length, height, and mental strength of the individual.A corresponding increase in the number of neurons, when you form and think a thought, means a greater absolute distance for the signal to travel. And it also means more travel time. In other words, the more neurons your thought system has, the more connections it has. And most neurons do not make physical connections with other neurons. But those neurons instead send electrical signals through neurotransmitter molecules (ions). They make use of the small spaces between nerve cells called synapses. This process takes much longer (at least 0.5 ms per synapse) than the continuous transmission of a signal within a single neuron. A particular thought or force in the mind can form and act in less than 150 ms.

These electrical properties in a single cell in the nervous system range from small to large to simple to economical. Although there are many different types of neurons in the brain, the same basic electrical principle underlies their function. When thoughts come into action, they generate electrical signals.

Neurotransmitters are chemical signals that carry messages from one neuron to the next nerve cell. Neurotransmitters are chemical messengers without which your body cannot function. Their important job is to carry chemical signals (messages) from one neuron to the next target cell. The next target cell could be another nerve cell, a muscle cell, or even a gland. It controls all of your nervous system movements, your thought processes, and your muscle and organ activity. To understand this more clearly, these neurotransmitters act on every thought and feeling you have. Your nerve cells send and receive information from all body sources.

Note: Although it is not possible to measure the speed of various thoughts, analyzing the time it takes to plan and complete actions provides important insights into how effectively the nervous system interacts with information, signals, and changes in movement and cognitive impairment. Thus its effectiveness ends with mental force.

Chapter 45

Nerves and neurotransmitters help you control what functions in your body:

Our brain's nervous system as a whole controls such functions. What are they specifically?

They are:

Thoughts

Memories

Learning

feelings

Heart rate and blood pressure

Breathing

sleep

Healing

mental stress

Muscle movements

Hormonal regulation

The five senses

Digestion

Hungry

Thirst

Nerve conductors control the above body functions and protect the human being. These actions are surprising to humans. This is because nerve conductors carry small electrical currents and information transmission is best carried out by small amounts of energy resulting in human impulses.

As many thoughts as you create in your mind, mental force will be created accordingly.Neurons in the brain cause the appropriate electrical signals for each thought. The endocrine glands of the brain, the organs of the brain, and the organs of the body produce various chemicals to suit each individual thought activity of the human being. Each of these chemicals has potential for each characteristic. A particular chemical product also has a particular philosophical nature. And for this there are molecules. And those molecules are based on unique properties, vibrations, waves, cooperation, and electricity. Therefore, when thoughts occur, when the chemical substance expresses its action, the human force for it is revealed, and then it is through neurons that the electric energy emerges from the brain, and this energy becomes a mind impulse and takes the form of time, cause, and action. Therefore, according to the thought of your mind, the neuron in the brain will have the speed m/s of the internal and external mental force. It is appropriate for each thought, the length of the body, and the relation of the particular organ to the neuron's velocity m/v is subject to or bound to change.

Chapter 46

What is Electromagnetism?

Definition of Electromagnetism: Electromagnetic force or

Electromagnetism is a kinetic branch of physics. It consists of the electromagnetic force that occurs between electrically charged particles. Electromagnetic force is one of the fundamental forces. It also exhibits electromagnetic fields such as magnetic fields, electric fields, and light.

Along with electricity and electromagnetism, the universe and we have acquired unified properties. Both of these are necessary for us to function. The electromagnetic force is also necessary for the Brahma instinct(force) and human instinct to work.

Chapter 47

Om is the word for mind and cosmic consciousness:

Definition of the cosmic consciousness word Om:

In the universe, the word AUM can refer to mind or consciousness. The word Om has the power to create anything. Therefore, Om is the word for the transcendental glory of cosmic consciousness. World's primary concept - by C .Poongavanam.

The glory of the sound Om:

Brahmarishi Mayan composed Aindram. His period is estimated to be around 10,000 years. He is known to be from Kumarikandam.

This book mentions about the universe, earth, and cosmic forces, i.e. five industries, five basic elements, directions of earth's place, etc. Mamuni Mayan is the creator of the Vastu Shastra system which has 64 squares. It is called Frog Maneri in Tamil and Manduka Mandala in Sanskrit.

Antecedent to concepts in Vastu Purusha Mandal are Mayan concepts.The absolute meaning of the source language. The subtle sound that originates from the source beyond all is permeating everywhere. The sound belonging to the space of knowledge released from that source deserves to be highlighted as 'Om'.

The sound of atoms is the best of the alphabet.

Description of:

The sound that rises at the most microscopic level is driven by the accumulation of atoms and evolves into the characteristic sound of writing.

The language itself, naturally gathered from the pure or transcendental space, spontaneously evolves into different languages in accordance with the nature of the respective places in the world and melts into a form of writing that arises in relation to one. The nature of writing can be explained in five stages: the ability to create sound and nature, the nature of form, the ability of color, and the ability of light. Writing is always up and running in the form of light and sound.

This Ongaram called Om became formless and form. From Ongaram, the world's living beings and five basic elements appeared. Om is the combination of the three letters A, U, M (AUM).- Thirumantram. Om is the first letter in the world so it is called Van letter.- Thirumoolar

To know this word Om is to know the secret of the universe.

Lord Shiva created the light Om from himself. Om is Pranavam. Om Tattva Masi (Thou art that) - There is a reference to the glory of the word Om in Sri Shiva Maha Puranam by Maharishi Veda Vyasa.

In the Vedas, the Mandukya Upanishad, the Bhagavad Gita, and other Indian texts describe its supreme glory. The Indian Siddhas, Rishis, Yogis, and Mahans realized the glory of the mantra Om. The word Om represents the soul. There is a lotus flower in the Om vibration. Buddhism also chants the mantra, Om.

(If properly pronounced, this OM will represent the whole phenomenon of sound production, and no other word can do this.) – Swami Vivekananda.

Note: The first vowel in most languages of the world is a. Surprisingly, the sound a and the letter a are included in the word Om.

Every sound produces every effect in the outer world. When the researchers arranged certain sounds in svarsthans (tunes) and played them repeatedly near a lake, due to the vibrations, the light shone on the water (water) as powder and then all the light particles were arranged in a specific shape.

Each type of svara (tunes) has a light form like this. From this scientific proof, it is possible to believe that one can get darshan of deity forms by means of Vedic mantra sounds. Light changes only sound in the external world. But also It spreads out in many other ways and has many different effects. Due to the Vedic sounds spreading in the outer atmosphere (atmosphere), there is great auspiciousness in the world. Such is the power of those mantras. Not only sound but its swaras dhana has power.

There are those who have seen exclusively in Thiruvanaikaval that even a tree in magical glory will sprout. The white novel tree called jambu is the local tree there. That is why the town is called Jambugeswaram. At a time when the local tree had fallen and only a single bark was keeping some life, Kanadukathan Chettiars did the work. Then they performed Ekadasa Rudrabhishekam for this tree. It loosened immediately due to magical power.

- Sri Kanchiparamachariyar. (This temple is located in Sri Rangam near Trichy in Tamil Nadu.)

We know that sound already passes into form through vibration. Again the modern periodic description phonon, in condensed-matter physics, is a unit of vibrational machinery arising from oscillating atoms within a crystal. Generally in all places of worship, there is a vibration. When chanting certain mantras with the right sound, there is a corresponding resonance. A phonon is a quantum of specific, vibrational mechanical energy. But, a photon is a quantum of electromagnetic or light energy. Both the phonon and the photon produce the effect of action in properly constructed temples in India. Space(akasha) has the characteristic of sound. Indian spiritual texts suggest this.

Chapter 48

Vibration creates light?

Yes, vibrations create light.

If the rate of vibration is very fast, about 500 million million times per second, then the resulting electromagnetic waves are visible to us as light. And it emits light in different colors.

When a monk chants AUM into a tonograph, this mantra produces an audio waveform image of the Sri Yantra, -tonography- Dr. Lawrence Blair

Dr. Lawrence Blair's research was evidenced in this sound-sensitive tonographer, which produced the AUM sound carefully chanted by a monk, revealing the Sri Yantra mount geometry. This is a hyper Sierpinski triangle sequence:

"Om", when correctly pronounced on the tonoscope, forms a circle "o' which is then filled with concentric squares and triangles. Finally the last traces of "m" are produced with the ending. A mechanistic geometrical expression of fearsome vibration. Dr. Lawrence Blair, Rhythms of Vision are Dynamic Forms of Faith Shogun, New York 1976. pp. 115

Chapter 49

An explanation of Om by Sri Sri Paramahamsa Yogananda:

The active manifestation of the all-pervading Christ (communal) consciousness, its witness in creation (revealed specialness (3:14), the Holy Spirit is the Word (John 1:1) and the Comforter (John 14:26) in the Bible).

Also referred to as "Om" in Hindu scriptures, this invisible divine power is the One Lord, sustaining all creation through vibration. The only cause is the substance, which is also understood as the active force. Through a special yoga meditation technique taught by the Yogada Satsang Society of India, the adept communicates with the Holy Spirit in rapture with Thetaravalan. The Holy Spirit, whom the Father will send in my name, will teach you everything and remind you of everything I told you. John (14:26)

By matter, the subtle construction of the universe, the intelligent cosmic vibration of God, arises from and is sustained by matter. The important properties of this vibration are sound and light. Om, the sound of God's creative vibrations, is referred to in Christian scriptures as Amen, the Holy Spirit, and the Word. Om is a

Sanskrit and Tamil word that represents the nature of the divine philosophy that creates and sustains all things. Beeja Oli: Cosmic Wave Vibration In the Vedas Ongaram became the holy word Hum of the Tibetans and Amen of the Muslims: Amen of the Egyptians, Greeks, Romans, Jews, and Christians. The world's leading religions assert that all created things emanate from the universal vibration energy of the word Om or Amen or the Holy Spirit. In the beginning was the Word. That word was from God. That Word was God. All things were made through Him (the Word or Om): that which was made was not made apart from Him. (John 1:1:3 Bible)

Amen in Hebrew means sure faith. Amen, the true witness and the beginning of God's creation, reveals the Bible. 8:14 The Bible, like the hum of a running motor, the sound of Om, the omnipresent sound, vibrates all living things in creation, every atom, to keep the cosmic motor running. It bears witness faithfully. -Man's Eternal Quest by Sri Sri Paramahamsa Yogananda has a wonderful description of Om.

According to the ancient sage Patanjali, God is the cosmic sound heard in meditation. Om is the creative word, the cogwheel of the cosmic machine, and the witness of divine presence. Om is a sound that can produce anything. It is this energy that travels in the waves of the universe and evolves into energy in all atoms. – Sri Sri Paramahamsa Yogananda – Autobiography of a Yogi – Tamil Book Page 18, Page 359.

Pranavam i.e. the light Om is the source of all sounds is a true concept realized by the true sages through their intuition. Just as snowdrops disappear when the sun shines, flowers bloom in their natural beauty, and darkness disappears when the light appears, so when the philosophers realize reality through their intuition, an ordinary person differs from the senses and gets the consciousness of the cosmic power.

A cynamatic instrument expresses sound vibrations as a pattern or visual representation. When chanting the word Om on this instrument, its vibration visualizes the shape of the Sri Yantra. Thus, the cosmic connection of Sri Yantra or Sri Chakra is explained scientifically.

Pronounced correctly, this Om represents the whole phenomenon of sound production, which no other word can do.

His (God's) manifest word is Om.

Swami Vivekananda (Book; Raja Yoga)

Swami Vivekananda:

Why is the glory of Om explained? When the word Om is uttered, the Sri Yantra is formed. The relationship between Om and Sri Chakra can be scientifically ascertained.

Chapter 50

Do our bodies have electricity?

Yes, our body has mild electricity. Electricity is everywhere in the human body, and our cells are specialized for communicating currents. Elements in our body like sodium, potassium, calcium, and magnesium have a specific charge. Almost all of our cells can use these charged elements, called ions, to generate electricity. Excited Cells to understand these electrical impulses, we need to look at our cells.

Excitable cells such as neurons (nerve cells) and muscle cells are polarized. The interior of each cell is negative. Externally, this negative potential difference is caused by uneven distribution. Ions on both sides of the cell membrane,The movement of these ions across the cell creates an electrical impulse across the membrane. This is known as functional capacity. Our nervous system uses these actions.

Einstein explained the energy of our electromagnetic wave light by saying that the energy of each particle of light is related to the frequency of the wave.Acts as both a particle and a wave.

Second, the photon is now considered a particle, a wave, and an excitation-type field. A quantum field likes an electromagnet

A field is a form of energy and potential that spreads throughout space. Energies that send signals around the body.

Thanks.

Notes:

1. Comments of Swami Vivekananda.

2. Commentaries of Paramahamsa Yogananda.

3. Arudberunch Jyoti Vallalar comments.

4. Comments of Sri Aravindar

5. UMPC website

6. Wikipedia

7. Google Websites

8. ncbi.nlm.nih.gov

9. Frontiersin.org

10. edx online course.

11. Theconversation.com

12. Plato.stanford.edu

13. Closer to truth

Technical terms

All matter and energy in the universe

Universal mind

Brahma force

Force

Mind force

The mind

Mind and matter

Mind vibration waves

Cosmic microcommunication

Consciousness

Subconscious

Awareness

Transcendence

Supernatural power

Feelings

Infinity

The observer

Thoughts

Existence

Philosophy

Metamorphosis

intelligent

Visibility

Visible things

Modern science

Motion

Energy

Speed

Elementray particles

Particles

Atoms

Nucleus

Proton (Positive)

Neutron (Neutral)

Electron negative

Signals

Neurons

Neurology of consciousness

Axons

Neurotransmitters

Molecules

Compounds

Chemical matters

Awaken the energy

Tradition

Brahma mind force and prana.

Brahma Force Correlation

Human mind force communication

Prana communication

Parabrahmam communication

Super Mind communication

Spatial communication

Natha level (vibration) communication

Atma Siddhi status communication

Man's mind force

Manas, Ahankara, buddhi, chitta

Conscious

Sub conscious mind

The highest level of consciousness or supermind.

Physical energy

Psychological power

Thought

Deep thinking

Actions

Powerful thought

Self-learning brings power

Mantra

Tantra

Yantra

Word

Writing

Form, Creative work

Meditation

Awareness

Transcendence
Spiritually exciting experiences

Pramananda

Breath

Controlling the external senses and reaching the

Intuitive stage

Changes occur in the human mind, body, brain

and nervous systems

Achieving a state of deep peace and silence

Enlightenment

Prayer

Ashta Siddhis

Memories

Curiosity about cosmic

Nature

Intellect

Reasoning

Brain and associated organs.

Space

Matter

Electromagnetic force.

Gravity force

Strong nuclear force

Weak nuclear force

Photon

Mind vibration

Vibration or sound

Light

Light wave

Wave

Wave length

Electromagnetic waves

Brain waves

Molecules

Chemical substances

Foods

Metaphysics (Mind and Matter)

Quantum Physics

Theory of Vibration

Resonance

Sound wave

Cosmic Energy

Microwave

Vital movement

Presumptive power

Super consciousness

Brain electrical energy

Displacement of mind is electricity

Electrochemical transmission

Photoreceptors

Conversion of electromagnetic

Transform photon

Electrical signals

Stimulate physiological process

Diffusion

Electrostatics

Electrostatic force

Frequencies

Metaphysics

Omniscient.

Sayings:

The universe, people, objects, thoughts, and events are mere images moving on the screen of pure consciousness, and that alone is real. Form and phenomena pass away, but consciousness remains forever.- Ramana Maharishi.

Thought waves are more powerful than the waves of speech and action. With every thought, word and action we create some waves in the atmosphere, but thought waves are especially penetrating, if we are cheerful, full of kindness and love. In the world, we receive love from every part. - Maharishi Mahesh Yogi. Science is the art of being and living. "Savitur", the sun, Super Mind, Or true of consciousness Symbolic.

Mental processes are actually physical processes in the sense that they undergo certain physical processes, intrinsically. What happened to such a thing is still a mystery. - Philosopher Thomas Nagel

An awareness or realization of an inner psychological or spiritual truth is an intuitively felt knowledge of something within one's inner self,

Also refers to the inward awareness of an external object, state, or fact - Webmaster's Third International Dictionary

Be alone, that's the secret, that's when ideas come. Nikola Tesla.

God will guide us in His time. Swami Vivekananda.

Shri Ramana Maharishi:

The mind is of thoughts bundle only.The thinker Because of Thoughts that arise. Thinker ego.Ego, if you search, automatically will disappear. Ego to Mind to the Same. Arrogance is when thoughts a rise it is basic thoughts.

Questioner: the mind looking for?

Shri Ramana Maharishi: Inside dive into. The mind from within arises that you now will know. Therefore inside Drowning searches for.

self the heart.

the heart Self Glowing.

the light from the heart arises

And the brain reaches,

of the mind Seat which.

the world by the mind is viewed, That is of the self Reflected by light.

It is of the mind with help is felt.

the mind Glowing when

It is the world knew.

It is itself Lightly When not,

It is the world don't know.

the mind If returned

of the light source towards,

objective Knowledge stops

And self only heartily shines

- Ramana Maharishi

Quantum mind or quantum consciousness is a group of hypotheses that propose that classical mechanics cannot explain consciousness. This suggests that quantum mechanical phenomena such as entanglement and superposition may play an important role in brain function and may explain consciousness.

Light is not made up of the physical light we are but of the spiritualized finger of prana intelligent life energy - Paramahamsa Yogananda

AUM is the Radiant Light. When this light spreads throughout the body, all is seen and then there is no desire to talk and see.- Sri Lahiri Mahasaya

According to Immanuel Kant (1787), discrete consciousness cannot be a succession of related ideas, but must at least be the experience of a conscious self situated in an objective world structured with respect to space, time, and reason.

Mother(Sri Aurobindo Ashram): Wherever and whenever a ray of consciousness has been possible since the beginning of the earth, I have been there.

who am I? Not the body because it rots; Not the mind, for the brain, will decay with the body; Not the personality, not the emotions, for these, too disappear with death - Ramana Maharishi.

The philosopher Plato saw consciousness as part of the ideal world. He thought that a person's consciousness creates mental images of concepts and ideas, saying that a person would only be imperfect if they tried to express those mental images in the real world.

What Ray Kurzweil means by considering non-biological intelligence is that basic consciousness is our own sense of our own awareness, subjective, and an object of scientific inquiry. It is the subject of an objective object of observation and then discernment from there.

Thank you.

www.ingramcontent.com/pod-product-compliance
Lightning Source LLC
LaVergne TN
LVHW041027150826
845672LV00001B/235

* 9 7 9 8 8 9 1 3 3 2 2 8 7 *